U.S. Immigration Policy

Other Books of Related Interest

Opposing Viewpoints Series

America's Great Divide
Diversity, Equity, and Inclusion
Genocide
Human Trafficking

At Issue Series

The Federal Budget and Government Spending
Immigration Reform
Open Borders

Current Controversies Series

America's Role in a Changing World
Globalization
Immigration, Asylum, and Sanctuary Cities
Nativism, Nationalism, and Patriotism

> "Congress shall make no law . . . abridging the freedom of speech, or of the press."
>
> *First Amendment to the U.S. Constitution*

The basic foundation of our democracy is the First Amendment guarantee of freedom of expression. The Opposing Viewpoints series is dedicated to the concept of this basic freedom and the idea that it is more important to practice it than to enshrine it.

U.S. Immigration Policy

Sarah Suozzi, Book Editor

Published in 2025 by Greenhaven Publishing, LLC
2544 Clinton Street,
Buffalo NY 14224

First Edition

Articles in Greenhaven Publishing anthologies are often edited for length to meet page requirements. In addition, original titles of these works are changed to clearly present the main thesis and to explicitly indicate the author's opinion. Every effort is made to ensure that Greenhaven Publishing accurately reflects the original intent of the authors. Every effort has been made to trace the owners of the copyrighted material.

Cover image: Grossinger/Shutterstock.com.

Cataloging-in-Publication Data

Names: Suozzi, Sarah, editor.
Title: U.S. immigration policy / edited by Sarah Suozzi.
Description: First edition. | New York : Greenhaven Publishing, 2025. | Series: Opposing viewpoints | Includes index.
Identifiers: ISBN 9781534510234 (pbk.) | ISBN 9781534510241 (library bound)
Subjects: LCSH: United States--Emigration and immigration--Government policy--Juvenile literature. | Immigrants--United States--Juvenile literature.
Classification: LCC JV6483.U87 2025 | DDC 325.73--dc23

Manufactured in the United States of America

Website: http://greenhavenpublishing.com

Contents

The Importance of Opposing Viewpoints 10
Introduction 13

Chapter 1: How is the Current Debate About Immigration Rooted in Our Nation's Past?

Chapter Preface 17

1. The United States Is Not "a Nation of Immigrants" 18
   Roxanne Dunbar-Ortiz
2. The Immigrant Population Is Shrinking 32
   Stephanie Kramer and Jeffrey S. Passel
3. U.S. Immigration Policy Is Constantly Changing 43
   Diana Roy, Clair Klobucista, and Amelia Cheatham
4. Facts and Figures About Unauthorized Immigrants Are Not Always Accurate 54
   Jeffrey S. Passel and Jens Manuel Krogstad

Periodical and Internet Sources Bibliography 62

Chapter 2: Is Immigration Detrimental to the United States?

Chapter Preface 65

1. Immigrants Are Not Hurting U.S.-Born Workers 66
   Daniel Costa and Heidi Shierholz
2. Many Opinions About Immigrants and the Economy Are Myths 72
   Gretchen Frazee
3. Immigrants Are Committing Fewer Crimes 79
   Transactional Records Access Clearinghouse
4. Citizenship for Undocumented Immigrants Would Boost U.S. Economic Growth 88
   Giovanni Peri and Reem Zaiour

Periodical and Internet Sources Bibliography 99

Chapter 3: Who Should Be Allowed to Immigrate?

Chapter Preface 102

1. What Legal Obligation Does the United States Have to Accept Refugees? 103
   Liam Thornton
2. Should the United States Adopt a Merit-Based Immigration System? 110
   Julia Gelatt and Jeremy L. Neufield
3. Viewpoints on the Treatment of Immigrants 116
   BBC News
4. Opinions on DACA Recipients and Other Immigrant Groups 121
   Jean Lantz Reisz
5. A Case Study of Immigrants From Northern Central America 126
   Jenny Villatoro and Matthew Rooney

Periodical and Internet Sources Bibliography 137

Chapter 4: Are the Current Pathways to Naturalization & Citizenship Sufficient for Today's Needs?

Chapter Preface 140

1. Trump's Plans for Tougher Border Enforcement Won't Necessarily Stop Migrants 141
   Katrina Burgess
2. How Americans View Immigration and Other Issues 146
   Pew Research Center
3. What History Tells Us About the Assimilation of Immigrants 153
   Ran Abramitzky
4. Asylum Seekers Need to be Treated Under Civil Rights Laws 160
   National Library of Medicine

Periodical and Internet Sources Bibliography **164**

For Further Discussion **166**
Organizations to Contact **168**
Bibliography of Books **172**
Index **174**

The Importance of Opposing Viewpoints

Perhaps every generation experiences a period in time in which the populace seems especially polarized, starkly divided on the important issues of the day and gravitating toward the far ends of the political spectrum and away from a consensus-facilitating middle ground. The world that today's students are growing up in and that they will soon enter into as active and engaged citizens is deeply fragmented in just this way. Issues relating to terrorism, immigration, women's rights, minority rights, race relations, health care, taxation, wealth and poverty, the environment, policing, military intervention, the proper role of government—in some ways, perennial issues that are freshly and uniquely urgent and vital with each new generation—are currently roiling the world.

If we are to foster a knowledgeable, responsible, active, and engaged citizenry among today's youth, we must provide them with the intellectual, interpretive, and critical-thinking tools and experience necessary to make sense of the world around them and of the all-important debates and arguments that inform it. After all, the outcome of these debates will in large measure determine the future course, prospects, and outcomes of the world and its peoples, particularly its youth. If they are to become successful members of society and productive and informed citizens, students need to learn how to evaluate the strengths and weaknesses of someone else's arguments, how to sift fact from opinion and fallacy, and how to test the relative merits and validity of their own opinions against the known facts and the best possible available information. The landmark series Opposing Viewpoints has been providing students with just such critical-thinking skills and exposure to the debates surrounding society's most urgent contemporary issues for many years, and it continues to serve this essential role with undiminished commitment, care, and rigor.

The key to the series's success in achieving its goal of sharpening students' critical-thinking and analytic skills resides in its title—

Opposing Viewpoints. In every intriguing, compelling, and engaging volume of this series, readers are presented with the widest possible spectrum of distinct viewpoints, expert opinions, and informed argumentation and commentary, supplied by some of today's leading academics, thinkers, analysts, politicians, policy makers, economists, activists, change agents, and advocates. Every opinion and argument anthologized here is presented objectively and accorded respect. There is no editorializing in any introductory text or in the arrangement and order of the pieces. No piece is included as a "straw man," an easy ideological target for cheap point-scoring. As wide and inclusive a range of viewpoints as possible is offered, with no privileging of one particular political ideology or cultural perspective over another. It is left to each individual reader to evaluate the relative merits of each argument—as they see it, and with the use of ever-growing critical-thinking skills—and grapple with their own assumptions, beliefs, and perspectives to determine how convincing or successful any given argument is and how the reader's own stance on the issue may be modified or altered in response to it.

This process is facilitated and supported by volume, chapter, and selection introductions that provide readers with the essential context they need to begin engaging with the spotlighted issues, with the debates surrounding them, and with their own perhaps shifting or nascent opinions on them. In addition, guided reading and discussion questions encourage readers to determine the authors' point of view and purpose, interrogate and analyze the various arguments and their rhetoric and structure, evaluate the arguments' strengths and weaknesses, test their claims against available facts and evidence, judge the validity of the reasoning, and bring into clearer, sharper focus the reader's own beliefs and conclusions and how they may differ from or align with those in the collection or those of their classmates.

Research has shown that reading comprehension skills improve dramatically when students are provided with compelling, intriguing, and relevant "discussable" texts. The subject matter of these collections could not be more compelling, intriguing, or urgently relevant to today's students and the world they are poised to inherit. The anthologized articles and the reading and discussion questions that are included with them also provide the basis for stimulating, lively, and passionate classroom debates. Students who are compelled to anticipate objections to their own argument and identify the flaws in those of an opponent read more carefully, think more critically, and steep themselves in relevant context, facts, and information more thoroughly. In short, using discussable text of the kind provided by every single volume in the Opposing Viewpoints series encourages close reading, facilitates reading comprehension, fosters research, strengthens critical thinking, and greatly enlivens and energizes classroom discussion and participation. The entire learning process is deepened, extended, and strengthened.

For all of these reasons, Opposing Viewpoints continues to be exactly the right resource at exactly the right time—when we most need to provide readers with the critical-thinking tools and skills that will not only serve them well in school but also in their careers and their daily lives as decision-making family members, community members, and citizens. This series encourages respectful engagement with and analysis of opposing viewpoints and fosters a resulting increase in the strength and rigor of one's own opinions and stances. As such, it helps make readers "future ready," and that readiness will pay rich dividends for the readers themselves, for the citizenry, for our society, and for the world at large.

Introduction

> *We are a nation of immigrants. We are the children and grandchildren and great-grandchildren of the ones who wanted a better life, the driven ones, the ones who woke up at night hearing that voice telling them that life in that place called America could be better.*
>
> — *Mitt Romney*

Ever since human beings evolved as species, we have explored the world, moving from place to place in search of the life we want—or believe we deserve. We have collected ourselves in myriad types of communities, from nomadic tribes to small villages to bustling metropolitan cities to large countries, bound together in groups by a common culture or heritage or belief system. Thus, we began identifying ourselves as "Us" and everyone else as "Them".

In time, our communities expanded, and we encountered "Them", resulting, in some cases, in the establishment of trade and diplomacy, and in others, war and conquest. Some people chose to leave their homes in favor of these new communities, drawn by new ideas or better business opportunities, or simply driven by a need for adventure, to discover something beyond what was familiar. Some groups left their homes to expand their territory by conquering those around them. Others fled as refugees from war, persecution, and deprivation, hoping to find in these new places a safe and peaceful life, where their needs could be met without too much struggle.

So, it can be said that people moving from one country to another, for whatever reason, is nothing new. Aside from the Indigenous peoples, everyone who currently lives in the United States is either an immigrant or the descendant of immigrants. (And arguably, even the Indigenous groups likely arrived in North America through nomadic means, which would simply make them the very first immigrants to this land.)

Though the Spanish, French, and English referred to themselves as "colonists" upon arriving on the shores of this continent, a colonist is simply another name for an immigrant who is trying to establish a new country in territory that is new to them. Most of our ancestors arrived on the shores of North America looking for a place where they could pursue whatever life they chose.

It makes sense that the United States needed to establish rules and procedures for those who wished to immigrate to this country. But some feel that, in the currently established laws and procedures governing immigration and naturalization, there is little room for compassion and humanitarianism. Some feel that the current legal routes to citizenship are too arduous, convoluted, and expensive, especially when so many of the people who are trying to come to the United States are doing so because they are fleeing poverty and violence.

Others feel that the rules aren't strict enough, the screening processes to keep out criminals aren't in-depth enough, and the newcomers are a strain on the resources of a country that are already quite stretched thin.

So where do we draw the line? Who should be allowed to pursue the American Dream of "life, liberty, and the pursuit of happiness" that was written about in the Declaration of Independence? How many obstacles or barriers on the pathway to citizenship are too many? Though the United States has a long history of immigration, should the country, at some point, close its borders and refuse entry to certain groups? And what should happen to those who have entered the country without following the established legal protocols?

The very timely debates surrounding the issues of documented versus undocumented immigration, open borders versus closed borders, and the way immigrants as a whole have been treated in the past and present are explored in *U.S. Immigration Policy* (Opposing Viewpoints), shedding light on this divisive and ongoing issue that affects politics, policies, economics, and more in the United States and, ultimately, around the world.

Chapter 1

How Is the Current Debate About Immigration Rooted in Our Nation's Past?

Chapter Preface

The United States has long had a reputation for being a country largely built by immigrants. Americans used to refer to their country as a "melting pot", a place where people of all cultures and heritages came together and were welcomed and encouraged to pursue whatever life path would make them happy.

The viewpoints in this chapter discuss the history of immigration in the United States and the traditions surrounding it. They also explore the difficulty of collecting accurate data regarding immigration, even in modern times. It is not always easy to get the full picture of immigration in the United States, and some of these viewpoints explain that challenge.

Is the United States still a nation of immigrants? Are Americans still a model for the rest of the world when it comes to welcoming strangers to their shores? Do they still live up to the promise engraved on the Statue of Liberty? Readers are asked to consider these questions as they explore viewpoints related to immigration policies of the past and present.

The viewpoints in this chapter offer insight into the history of immigration and the treatment of immigrants in the United States. These viewpoints reflect the discussions and debates at the heart of the issue of immigration policy throughout American history. These discussions and debates are still a major part of American life and government today.

Viewpoint 1

> *"...multiculturalism is the mechanism for avoiding acknowledgement of settler colonialism."*

The United States is Not "a Nation of Immigrants"

Roxanne Dunbar-Ortiz

In the following viewpoint, Roxanne Dunbar-Ortiz argues that the United States is not, and has never been, a nation of immigrants, but rather a country made up of colonized settler states. She discusses how the processes of Americanization and historical review has clouded and camouflaged this issue.

As you read, consider the following questions:

1. Is there, in fact, a difference between an "immigrant" and a "settler" and, if so, what is the importance of that distinction?
2. How has the existence of Indigenous Native peoples and the "Thanksgiving Myth" clouded or complicated analysis of this issue?
3. According to the author, how have immigrants themselves contributed to the mis-classification of the United States as a "nation of immigrants"?

"The United States is Not 'a Nation of Immigrants,'" Roxanne Dunbar-Ortiz, Boston 50 Review, August 16, 2021. Reprinted by permission.

The United States has never been "a nation of immigrants." It has always been a settler state with a core of descendants from the original colonial settlers, that is, primarily Anglo-Saxons, Scots, Irish, and Germans. The vortex of settler colonialism sucked immigrants through a kind of seasoning process of Americanization—not as rigid and organized as the "seasoning" of Africans, which rendered them into human commodities, but effective nevertheless.

In the 1960s, U.S. historians were having to adjust the historical narrative of the white republic and progress in response to Black civil rights demands for a reckoning about racism. But in the process of those adjustments and reforms, the settler state was never a subject of debate. Mahmood Mamdani writes:

> If America's greatest social successes have been registered on the frontier of race, the same cannot be said of the frontier of colonialism. If the race question marks the cutting edge of American reform the native question highlights the limits of that reform. The thrust of American struggles has been to deracialize but not to decolonize. A deracialized America still remains a settler society and a settler state.

Attempts to "include" Native peoples as victims of racism further camouflages settler colonialism and constitutes a type of social genocide. The U.S. polity has been trying to rid itself of Indigenous nations since first settlement. Four hundred years later, multiculturalism is the mechanism for avoiding acknowledgment of settler colonialism. Mamdani correctly observes that the very existence of Indigenous nations "constitutes a claim on land and therefore a critique of settler sovereignty and an obstacle to the settler economy."

Multiculturalism was the response to civil rights demands, which required a revised narrative of U.S. history. For this scheme to work—and affirm U.S. historical progress—Indigenous nations and communities had to be left out of the picture or somehow woven into the story. As territorially and treaty-based peoples in North America, they do not fit the grid of multiculturalism, but were included by transforming them into an inchoate, oppressed racial group, while oppressed Mexican Americans and colonized Puerto Ricans were dissolved into another such group, variously called "Hispanic" or "Latino," and more recently "Latinx." The multicultural approach emphasized the "contributions" of oppressed groups and immigrants to the United States' presumed greatness. Indigenous peoples were thus credited with contributing corn, beans, buckskin, log cabins, parkas, maple syrup, canoes, hundreds of place names, ecology, Thanksgiving, and even contributing to the Constitution the concepts of democracy and federalism.

This idea of the gift-giving Indian helping to establish and enrich the development of the United States is a screen that obscures the fact that the very existence of the country is a result of the looting of an entire continent and its resources, reducing the Indigenous population, and forcibly relocating and incarcerating them in reservations. The fundamental unresolved issues of Indigenous lands, treaties, and sovereignty could not but scuttle the premises of multiculturalism for Native Americans. Multiculturalism persisted into the neoliberal twenty-first century, culminating in widespread "diversity" training, the coining of a new term, "people of color," and the production of *Hamilton*, which not only erased the Indigenous peoples and African slavery but also turned the white founding fathers, who authored a Constitution that recognized only white people as citizens, into brown and Black men.

The Thanksgiving myth obscures the fact that the very existence of the country is a result of the looting of an entire continent, reducing the Indigenous population, and forcibly relocating and incarcerating them in reservations.

The Black Power and women's liberation movements of the 1960s gave birth to "identity politics," which saw the coalescence of Mexican American youth as Chicanos, Native American Red Power, and a trans-Asian Pacific American identity. A generation that came to adulthood in the 1960s who could not speak Chinese or

Spanish, as their immigrant parents felt it might hold their children back, embraced bilingualism. European immigrants or second-generation U.S. Americans, whose parents and grandparents had strived so hard to be considered white, saw the cultural power of whiteness diminishing and began to hyphenate their identity as Polish American, Italian American, and Irish American, while white Appalachians and New Mexico Hispano settlers claimed indigeneity. Instead of the melting pot that erased ethnic heritage, there was talk of patchwork quilts and threads, multiculturalism and diversity.

Immigration in the new millennium looked different from past immigration in that Asia was the major region of origin rather than Latin America, at 41 percent of all immigrants, with 38.9 percent from Latin America, primarily Mexico. Between 2000 and 2017, the top three countries of origin were China, India, and Pakistan, followed by the Philippines. Most importantly, nearly half of the new immigrants were college graduates, many with advanced degrees. They were not heading only to Silicon Valley or other high-tech industrial centers, nor were they, as had immigrants in the past, settling mainly in the large coastal cities. Rather, they could be found in the Deep South, the Great Plains, the intermountain West, and Appalachia. In North Dakota, where immigrants represented about 4 percent of residents, immigrant numbers increased by 87 percent after 2010, while West Virginia and South Dakota increased in foreign- born residents by a third, and Kentucky and Tennessee by over a fifth. And many of these immigrants—some of whom were refugees, others undocumented—came not only from South, West, and East Asia but also from African and Arab countries, the Caribbean, and Central and South America. Like the Chinese and Mexican immigrants before them, they experienced racialization, thereby lacking a key element of settler colonialism: potential whiteness. They or their children could become thoroughly Americanized but still remain contingent, even the son of a Kenyan who was twice elected president but whose citizenship was questioned by a substantial part of the population, including by the president who followed him.

The trend of "third world" immigration began with the 1965 immigration law, but accelerated with the Western nations' retreat from funding and supporting decolonization and nation-building, which accelerated debt, austerity, and famine, and, in the case of the United States, fronting and arming counterinsurgencies to prevent authentic self-determination, making the countries of origin unlivable. Suketu Mehta immigrated with his family from Mumbai at age fourteen. A prize-winning author and associate professor of journalism at New York University, he observes in his book This Land Is Our Land: An Immigrant's Manifesto (2019) that "they are here because you were there." He corrects the idea that immigrants clamor to leave their homelands to pursue the American Dream.

> When migrants move, it's not out of idle fancy, or because they hate their homelands, or to plunder the countries they come to, or even (most often) to strike it rich. They move—as my grandfather knew—because the accumulated burdens of history have rendered their homelands less and less habitable.

Mehta questions the presumed U.S. reader to consider how frequently the U.S. military has gone over its southern border or into the Caribbean or Southeast Asia, or gone over the borders of Iraq or Afghanistan.

> The United States has not acted lawfully with other nations, including the Native American nations on its soil, through most of the nineteenth and twentieth centuries. How can it now expect the human victims of that enormous illegality to obey the laws of the United States and stay home or wait thirty years for a visa to rejoin their families?

Mehta proposes that the United States (and other Western countries) pay reparations:

> If the rich countries don't want the poor countries to migrate, then there's another solution. Pay them what they're owed. Pay the costs of colonialism, of the wars you imposed on them, of the inequality you've built into the world order, and the carbon you've put into the atmosphere. Settle the account, and the creditors will have no reason to come to your house. Reparations or migration: choose.

Mehta points out that migrants, as we have seen with Mexican and Philippine migrants, send back to their home countries some $600 billion in remittances every year, amounting to four times more than all the Western foreign aid and a hundred times more than the amount of all debt relief. In addition to the ruin wrought by European colonization and U.S. wars and interventions, plus extreme economic inequality, Mehta sees catastrophic climate change as a source of mass migrations in the twenty-first century, displacing far more people than were displaced at the end of World War II. By 2050 up to 30 percent of the planet's surface could be unlivable desert, forcing a 1.5 billion people into migration. In Bangladesh alone, 20 million people could be forced out due to rising sea levels, and by the end of the century, the lands of 650 million people could be underwater. Obviously, rich countries will be increasingly a destination for desperate migrants and need to plan to provide assistance, not build walls or increase mass deportations.

Although he is critical of U.S. imperialism and immigration policies, Mehta does not acknowledge settler colonialism and the immigrant's role in perpetuating it.

Mehta's manifesto is deeply researched and insightful and should be a refreshing rejoinder to the American Dream and bootstrap stories that many immigrants, and more Anglo settlers, are asked to tell themselves. But Mehta does characterize the United States as "a nation of immigrants" that does not live up to that aspiration. Although he is critical of U.S. imperialism and immigration policies, Mehta does not acknowledge settler colonialism and the immigrant's role in perpetuating it. The Native is mentioned as an oppressed demographic, but otherwise is invisible.

Moroccan Muslim immigrant Laila Lalami, a prize-winning novelist, writer, and university professor, aptly titled her 2020 book Conditional Citizens: On Belonging in America. She was born in Rabat, Morocco; was educated in Morocco, Great Britain, and the United States; married a U.S. citizen; and was naturalized in 2000. Lalami relates that she had no trouble with the citizenship test, because before she came to the United States, she had taken courses on U.S. history, had studied its literature, and had become acquainted with the culture.

She discovered quickly on arrival in the United States that the Americans she met knew nothing of her country's history or culture, although they knew the racist caricatures of Arabs and Muslims. As an immigrant, a woman, an Arab, and a Muslim, Lalami was made to feel like a "conditional citizen." That feeling escalated with the Al Qaeda attacks on the World Trade Center and the Pentagon on September 11, 2001, because the nineteen airplane hijackers were all Muslim, all but one from U.S.-allied Saudi Arabia. The U.S. revenge war in Afghanistan was framed as anti-Muslim—as was the 2003 invasion of Iraq, where, in fact, there was little hardline Islam and no terror attacks by Iraqis. As that heated anti-Muslim period abated somewhat, Lalami was disturbed by the citizen birthright rhetoric that began with the presidency of Barack Obama, who was the target of the "birther" craze claiming that Obama was a secret Muslim actually born in Kenya, making him ineligible for the presidency. The instigator of this false charge, real-estate mogul Donald Trump, ascended to the presidency in 2017 largely on birtherism and his attacks on Muslim and Mexican immigrants. As one of his first acts as president, he banned visitors and immigrants from some Muslim-majority countries by executive order. In a chapter titled "Assimilation," Lalami insightfully discusses the U.S. nineteenth-century programs to erase the languages, cultures, and social relations practiced by

Indigenous peoples, citing the mandatory boarding schools that took Native children from their families and communities. She is alert to that process of Americanization being demanded of immigrants to the United States as well. While making common cause between immigrants, especially immigrants of color, and Native Americans, she does not interrogate the role of immigrants in perpetuating settler colonialism. The instability caused by the conditionality of citizenship that Lalami expresses is a barrier to the immigrant's ability to see the role they may play in normalizing settler colonialism.

Dean Itsuji Saranillio writes that migration to a settler-colonial state is fraught because Native land and resources "are under political, ecological, and spiritual contestation," which means that immigrant communities can duplicate a colonial system initiated by white settlers. "This is particularly so since the avenues laid out for success and empowerment are paved over Native lands and sovereignty." Saranillio is referencing Hawaii, where the Native Hawaiian (Kanaka Maoli) population is 10 percent, and Asians, primarily Japanese and Filipino, make up the majority at nearly 40 percent, while the U.S. settler population is just under 30 percent. Although the United States occupied Hawai'i and overthrew its constitutional monarchy as a prelude to the invasion and occupation of the Philippines, Guam, and other Pacific islands in the late nineteenth century, Congress long considered Hawai'i to be unqualified for statehood, because it was "Asiatic." Indeed, this was the reason that none of the Pacific territories the United States held were considered for statehood. But the resident U.S. citizen settlers in Hawai'i, who had been uninvited businessmen and missionaries even before the U.S. occupation, desired statehood and lobbied hard for it.

Without consciousness of and resistance to the pull of Americanism, the migrant can passively contribute to the continued settler-colonial order.

These wealthy U.S. businessmen settlers operated vast sugar and pineapple plantations in Hawai'i and recruited migrant agricultural workers from Japan and the Philippines, who then came to make up a large part of the foreign residents, outnumbering the indigenous Kanaka Maoli. Saranillio detects the hidden motive for U.S. support of Hawai'i statehood:

> In the 1940s and 1950s, when decolonization was transforming an international order and criticism of Western imperialism was the dominant international sentiment, Cold Warrior ideologues realized that Hawai'i's multiracial population had ideological value in winning the 'hearts and minds' of newly decolonized nations. . . . The US liberal multicultural discourse—articulated through a multicultural 'nation of immigrants' narration—helped achieve seemingly permanent control of Hawai'i through statehood while creating a multicultural image of the United States that facilitated US ambitions for global hegemony.

Hawai'i became a state in 1959, despite the fact that as an island subjected to Western colonization, it was eligible for independence under international law. In 1946 Hawai'i was deemed a non-self-governing territory and placed on the UN List of Non-Self-Governing Territories, but was unilaterally removed from that list in 1959 when the U.S. government reported to the UN that Hawai'i had achieved self-government. The same applied to Alaska. The Kanaka Maoli of Hawai'i, Alaskan Inuit, American Indians, and their allies continue to pursue independence.

Asian American scholar Iyko Day challenges a binary theory of settler colonialism regarding non-European immigration. "While scholarship on the settler-Indigenous dialectic has been tremendously valuable, it often falls short of clarifying the role that nonwhite migration plays within such a framework or how it intersects with other aspects of white supremacy." Day rightly objects to the settler status collapsing all migrants into a group of "occupiers." Chickasaw scholar Jodi Byrd extends the term "arrivant," which refers to enslaved Africans transported against their will, to refugees and immigrants forced out of their homelands; that is, "those people forced into the Americas through the violence of European and Anglo-American colonialism and imperialism around the globe."

The desire to relieve the non-European migrant or descendants of enslaved Africans from responsibility is understandable but not sustainable if the settler-colonial foundation is to be eradicated.

But the migrant forced into migration to the United States or other states structured on settler colonialism—Canada, New Zealand, Australia, Israel—is susceptible, as Saranillio points out, to the ideology of settler colonialism, which in the United States is imprinted in the content of patriotism and Americanism. Without consciousness of and resistance to this pull, the migrant can passively contribute to the continued settler-colonial order. The desire to relieve the non-European migrant or descendants of enslaved Africans from responsibility is understandable but not sustainable if the settler-colonial foundation is to be eradicated—that is, the decolonization of the entire apparatus of the settler state. What would that entail? U.S. social movement organizer Clare Bayard likely captured the dilemma for most non-Indigenous activists in the United States, saying: "The difficulty that a lot of non-Native people have in imagining what unsettling would look like in this country is that it's not seen as a political possibility. We can't even imagine what that would look like—how do we do that?"

The claim that the United States is "a nation of immigrants" is the benevolent version of U.S. nationalism. The ugly underside is the panic of enemy invasion. In the Supreme Court ruling on a case challenging the Chinese Exclusion Act of 1893 (Fong Yue Ting v. United States), Justice Horace Gray wrote:

> the presence of foreigners of a different race in this country . . . [is] dangerous to its peace and security, their exclusion is not to

> be stayed because at the time there are no actual hostilities with the nation of which the foreigners are subject. The existence of war would render the necessity of the proceeding only more obvious and pressing.

The view that migrants are proxies for foreign troops dates back to the founders of the United States and the Alien and Sedition Acts. Immigration historian Mae Ngai sees the character of U.S. nationalism as the driver of its fear of immigrants:

> Americans want to believe that immigration into the United States proves the universality of the nation's liberal democratic principles; we resist examining the role that American world power has played in the global structures of migration. We like to believe that our immigration policy is generous, but we also resent the demands made upon us by others and we think we owe outsiders nothing.

The United States is under the illusion that it is surrounded by enemies, that it must strike first, savagely, with preemptive action, even war. Historian Walter Hixson writes of the "boomerang of savagery," arguing that "the history of American settler colonialism, and the indiscriminate violence that it entailed, burrowed into US national identity and foreign relations." As Native nations resisted encroachment, starting with the first English settlement in 1607, the traumatized settlers hardened the mythology of providential destiny, fueling indiscriminate carnage, which was even more hideous in the Plymouth and Massachusetts Bay Colonies, escalating exponentially until total conquest was complete by 1900. Hixson writes:

> Americans thus internalized a propensity for traumatic, righteous violence, and a quest for total security, which came to characterize a series of future conflicts. Violence against Indians, replete with demonizing colonial discourse and indiscriminate killing, established a foundation for virulent national campaigns against external enemies across the sweep of American history.

This is the chief characteristic of U.S. nationalism, and it is similar to other settler states, such as Australia, New Zealand, Canada, Northern Ireland, and twentieth-century copycat settler states Israel and the now-defunct Afrikaner apartheid regime in South Africa. But only the United States became an unparalleled capitalist state and military machine. Unlike those other states—whose damage, damaging as it is, remains mostly local or regional—the United States rules the seas and skies, with the futures of humanity and Earth itself at stake.

"Violence against Indians, replete with demonizing colonial discourse and indiscriminate killing, established a foundation for virulent national campaigns against external enemies."

Immigrants and refugees from U.S. wars, including Mexicans from the war that created the southern border, have an important role to play if there is to be change. Viet Thanh Nguyen observes that "identity politics" is treated as a slur, something to be avoided. It appears to be the one thing that many on the left and the solid right agree on. Nguyen writes, "To have no identity at all is the privilege of whiteness, which is the identity that pretends not to have an identity, that denies how it is tied to capitalism, to race, and to war." He calls on minorities to dissent from the terms that a regime of whiteness offers: "They must call forth anger and rage, demand solidarity and revolution, critique whiteness, domination, power, and all the faces of the war machine," and in particular for Southeast Asians, insist that "the war that defines them in America is not only their war, but a war made by white people, a war that is not an aberration but a manifestation of a war machine that would prefer refugees to think of their stories as immigrant stories. . . . We must also tell the war stories that made ghosts and made us ghosts, the war stories that brought us here."

The Meaning of "The New Colossus"

Not like the brazen giant of Greek fame,
With conquering limbs astride from land to land;
Here at our sea-washed, sunset gates shall stand
A mighty woman with a torch, whose flame
Is the imprisoned lightning, and her name
Mother of Exiles. From her beacon-hand
Glows world-wide welcome; her mild eyes command
The air-bridged harbor that twin cities frame.
"Keep, ancient lands, your storied pomp!" cries she
With silent lips. "Give me your tired, your poor,
Your huddled masses yearning to breathe free,
The wretched refuse of your teeming shore.
Send these, the homeless, tempest-tost to me,
I lift my lamp beside the golden door!"

-Emma Lazarus

When Lazarus wrote this poem in 1883, immigrants were entering the United States in great numbers, including Italians, French, Greeks, and Russian-Jewish refugees, among other. And sure enough, "The New Colossus" is itself a multicultural amalgam: an Italian sonnet written by a Jewish-American woman, celebrating a statue forged in France, and contrasting it with another in ancient Greece.

This new colossus, Lazarus insists, is "not like" the Greek Colossus, domineering and male, which in the third century BCE stood at the harbor of the island of Rhodes, like some conquering warrior and guardian. No, this statue holds a beacon in her hand, signaling mothering less than "world-wide welcome." Her name is "Mother of Exiles." She is unarmed, a light in one hand and a votive tablet in the other. Such tablets were common in ancient Greece for inscribing prayers, or in any case aspirations – and on this particular tablet is the date the United States formally broke from English rule: July 4, 1776. It's as if she says, *We aspire to be free – now come, all you who yearn for freedom*.

She is herself the personification of freedom, of course, the Roman goddess Libertas. But compare her with Eugéne Delacroix's 1830 painting, *Liberty Leading the People*, in which Libertas carries a battle flag and gun. No, this version of Libertas is unarmed, a powerful, poised image of peace and hospitality. In the decades since the poem's writing, including recent days, American "nativists" (so-called!) have sought to recast her as a guard keeping people out. But Lazarus' poem stands as a ringing rebuke to this idea. This isn't the old colossus, but rather a new one: far from keeping people out, Lady Liberty – that "mighty woman with a torch, whose flame / is the imprisoned lightning" – is welcoming us in.

"The New Colossus," by Emma Lazarus, SALT, June 24, 2024.

> *"Even as the nation's immigrant population has declined in recent months – a change that may be partly artificial due to a declining survey response rate among immigrants – the U.S. is home to more immigrants than any other country."*

The Immigrant Population Is Shrinking

Stephanie Kramer and Jeffrey S. Passel

In this article, Stephanie Kramer and Jeffrey S. Passel present statistics in favor of the argument that immigration to the United States is currently on the decline, and discuss how several recent policy changes have affected the U.S. immigrant population.

As you read, consider the following questions:

1. Why do the authors specifically note the declining survey response rate among immigrants while discussing the current data?
2. How much do immigrants' places of origin impact their ability to assimilate into U.S. culture?
3. How has U.S. immigration law impacted the types of people who have immigrated in the last 200 years?

"What the data says about immigrants in the U.S.," Pew Research Center, Washington, D.C. (September 27, 2024)

After more than 50 years of rapid growth, the nation's immigrant population is now in decline.

In January 2025, 53.3 million immigrants lived in the United States – the largest number ever recorded. In the ensuing months, however, more immigrants left the country or were deported than arrived. By June, the country's foreign-born population had shrunk by more than a million people, marking its first decline since the 1960s.

A new Pew Research Center analysis of Census Bureau data finds that, as of June 2025:

- 51.9 million immigrants lived in the U.S.
- 15.4% of all U.S. residents were immigrants, down from a recent historic high of 15.8%.
- 19% of the U.S. labor force were immigrants, down from 20% and by over 750,000 workers since January.

Starting in mid-2024, several policy changes have affected the U.S. immigrant population:

- In June 2024, President Joe Biden announced new restrictions on asylum applications, leading to a sharp decline in border encounters with immigrants seeking asylum protections.
- In his first 100 days since returning to the White House in January, President Donald Trump took 181 executive actions on immigration to curtail the arrival of new immigrants and deport noncitizen immigrants. The full effects of these policies remain to be seen, but already they are contributing to a declining immigrant population – especially the unauthorized immigrant population.

How we did this

Pew Research Center conducted this analysis to answer common questions about immigration to the United States and the U.S. immigrant population. The immigrant or foreign-born population consists of people born outside of the United States or its territories who are not U.S. citizens at birth.

Estimates for 2025 are from Pew Research Center tabulations of the Census Bureau's monthly Current Population Surveys, accessed through IPUMS. The Current Population Survey's June 2025 estimate was the most recent available as of July 31. Note that the recent downward trend in the estimated U.S. immigrant population may in part be due to technical reasons such as declining CPS survey participation among immigrants.

Data on characteristics and legal status of U.S. immigrants in 2023 comes from Center analysis of augmented and supplemented 2023 American Community Survey data (IPUMS). The analysis also includes historical data from decennial censuses.

The estimates presented in this research for 2023 are the Center's latest. The 2023 ACS was supplemented to take into account the Census Bureau's 2024 revisions to their population estimates based on increased levels of net international migration. Read the methodology of this report for more details.

Comparative data on other countries around the world comes from the United Nations' migrant stock and overall population estimates for 2024.

Pew Research Center regularly publishes research on the U.S. immigrant population and international migration trends. Here are answers to some key questions about U.S. immigrants, based on the most recent detailed data available. (In some cases, this data is from mid-2023.)

How many people in the U.S. are immigrants?

As of June 2025, 51.9 million immigrants lived in the U.S., making up 15.4% of the nation's population. This was down from January, when there were a record 53.3 million immigrants in the U.S., accounting for 15.8% of the country's population – the highest percentage on record.

Even as the nation's immigrant population has declined in recent months – a change that may be partly artificial due to a declining survey response rate among immigrants – the U.S. is home to more immigrants than any other country.

As of 2024, the second-largest immigrant population is in Germany, numbering around 17 million, according to the latest estimates from the United Nations.

While the U.S. is home to the largest *number* of immigrants, dozens of countries (including Germany) have a higher *proportion* of immigrants in their populations than the U.S. does. In neighboring Canada, for example, immigrants account for 22% of the population. And in the United Arab Emirates, about three-quarters of all residents were born elsewhere.

Where are U.S. immigrants from?

As of mid-2023 – the latest year for which detailed data is available – more than 11 million U.S. residents were born in Mexico, representing 22% of all immigrants nationally. The second-largest immigrant group was from India (3.2 million, or 6%), followed by China (3 million, or 6%), the Philippines (2.1 million, or 4%) and Cuba (1.7 million, or 3%).

About half of all U.S. immigrants (52%, or 26.7 million people) were born in Latin America. In addition to the millions of migrants from Mexico and Cuba, more than a million hail from El Salvador (1.6 million), Guatemala (1.4 million), the Dominican Republic (1.4 million), Colombia (1.2 million), Honduras (1.1 million) and Venezuela (1.1 million).

After Latin America, Asia is the second-largest region of birth for U.S. immigrants. In 2023, around a quarter of all immigrants (27%, or nearly 14 million people) were born in Asia.

As of 2023, there were about 11 million immigrants from every other world region combined, accounting for 22% of the U.S. foreign-born population: 10% were born in Europe, 5% in sub-Saharan Africa, 4% in the Middle East-North Africa region, and 2% in Canada or another North American country (a category that includes Bermuda and some smaller countries).

How have immigrants' origins changed in recent years?

An unprecedented number of immigrants – more than 11 million – arrived in the U.S. between 2020 and 2025. That included more than 3 million in 2023 alone, the largest annual total ever recorded, according to a Center analysis of government data sources.

Alongside this increase, immigrants' origin regions have also shifted, with a growing share coming from South America and Europe and a declining share coming from Asia and sub-Saharan Africa.

Between 2021 and 2023, 20% of newly arrived immigrants were from South America, up from 13% in the period between 2015 and 2019. Another 12% of new arrivals between 2021 and 2023 were from Europe or Canada, up from 9% in the earlier period.

At the same time, 24% of new arrivals between 2021 and 2023 were from South and East Asia, down from 29% in 2015-19. And 5% of new arrivals between 2021 and 2023 involved people from sub-Saharan Africa, down from 8% in 2015-19.

Mexico was the largest origin country for immigrants who arrived between 2021 and 2023. About 11% of immigrants who came to the U.S. during this period were born in Mexico. Rounding out the top five countries of origin for immigrants who arrived during this period were India (8%), Venezuela (7%), Cuba (6%) and Colombia (5%).

Throughout this period, unauthorized immigrants accounted for most new immigrant arrivals, with many coming from Central and South America.

How have immigration flows changed over the longer term?

Since 1965, more than 76 million immigrants have come to the U.S.

Before then, U.S. immigration law favored immigrants from Northern and Western Europe and mostly barred immigration from Asia. The 1965 Immigration and Nationality Act opened up immigration from Asia and Latin America. The Immigration Act of

1990 further increased legal immigration and allowed immigrants from more countries to enter the U.S. legally.

Immigration flows after 1965 have been larger and come from different and more countries than earlier flows:

- From 1840 to 1889, about 90% of U.S. immigrants came from Europe, including about 70% from Germany, Ireland and the United Kingdom.
- Almost 90% of the immigrants who arrived from 1890 to 1919 also came from Europe. But their origins were largely different as nearly 60% came from Italy, Austria-Hungary and Russia-Poland.
- Since 1965, about half of U.S. immigrants have come from Latin America, with about a quarter from Mexico alone. About another quarter have come from Asia. Large numbers have come from China, India and the Philippines.

Today, Mexico remains the largest origin country among U.S. immigrants. However, immigration from Mexico has slowed since 2007, and the Mexican-born population in the U.S. has since dropped. The Mexican share of the U.S. immigrant population declined from 29% in 2010 to 22% in 2023.

What is the legal status of immigrants in the U.S.?

As of 2023, 46% of immigrants were naturalized U.S. citizens. Nearly a quarter (23%) were lawful permanent residents, often referred to as "green card holders," and another 4% were lawful temporary residents who were permitted to stay in the U.S. for a limited period of time, usually for work or study. The remaining immigrants in the U.S. fell into the "unauthorized" category and constituted 27% of all U.S. immigrants.

Who are unauthorized immigrants?

Unauthorized immigrants are those without full legal status. As of 2023, this population hit a new record high of 14 million. Within this group, about 6 million (or a little more than 40%) had some form of temporary protection from deportation, with some also having a permit to work in the U.S.

Among the unauthorized immigrants with some deportation protections were 2.6 million asylum applicants; 700,000 people who entered the U.S. legally after receiving parole; 700,000 victims of crime and violence; 650,000 people with Temporary Protected Status (TPS), a program available to immigrants from countries facing war, natural disasters and other crises; and 600,000 immigrants who were brought to the U.S. illegally as children and are enrolled in the Deferred Action for Childhood Arrivals (DACA) program.

Another 1 million migrants encountered U.S. Border Patrol before being released into the U.S., typically with an order to appear in immigration court. These immigrants have had more limited protections from deportation while their cases are being resolved.

Immigrants in these groups are included as part of the "unauthorized" population because their deportation protections are temporary and can quickly change. For example, the Trump administration has rescinded deportation protections and work permits for about 500,000 immigrants from Cuba, Haiti, Nicaragua and Venezuela who entered the U.S. legally.

The remaining unauthorized immigrants in the U.S. as of 2023 (about 8 million) had neither legal status nor temporary protection from deportation.

This year, policy and enforcement changes likely contributed to a decline in the unauthorized immigrant population between January and June. Border crossings have fallen further, reaching lows not seen since the 1960s. Immigration arrests and deportations have increased. And a growing number of immigrants have lost deportation protections, with some likely leaving the country voluntarily.

Do all lawful immigrants choose to become U.S. citizens?

Immigrants who are lawful permanent residents and meet other requirements can apply to become U.S. citizens through the naturalization process. During the 2024 fiscal year, 818,500 immigrants became U.S. citizens through naturalization.

Millions of lawful permanent residents are currently eligible to become U.S. citizens but have not applied for naturalization.

How many immigrants are working in the U.S.?

Between January and June 2025, the number of immigrants living and working in the U.S. declined. But recent figures by legal status are not yet available.

In 2023, the most recent year with complete data, 33 million immigrants were in the U.S. workforce, including about 23 million lawful immigrants and 10 million unauthorized immigrants.

Nearly one-in-five workers (19%) were immigrants in 2023, up from 15% two decades earlier. This share increased steadily since at least 1995, when they made up 12% of the labor force.

About 2% of adult immigrants, including noncitizens, are currently serving in the military or served in the past.

Where do most U.S. immigrants live?

In 2023, most of the nation's 51.8 million immigrants lived in just four states. California was home to 11.3 million immigrants, or 28.4% of the national total. Texas had the second-largest immigrant population with over 6 million foreign-born residents, followed by Florida (5.4 million) and New York (5.0 million).

A majority of immigrants lived in only 12 metropolitan areas. The New York City metropolitan area was home to the largest population, accounting for 13% of all immigrants. The Los Angeles and Miami metro areas also had particularly large immigrant populations, with 9% and 6% of all U.S. immigrants, respectively.

How educated are immigrants?

Overall, immigrants in the U.S. had lower levels of educational attainment than their U.S.-born counterparts in 2023.

- 24% of immigrant adults ages 25 and older had not completed high school, compared with 7% of the U.S.-born population.
- However, immigrants were as likely as the U.S. born to have a bachelor's degree or higher (36% each).

Educational attainment among immigrants varies widely based on their region of origin:

- Only 11% of Central American immigrants hold a bachelor's degree or higher. By comparison, 36% of U.S.-born adults have this level of education.
- Immigrants from Asia, Europe, the Middle East-North Africa region, sub-Saharan Africa and other North American countries are *more* likely than the U.S. born to have at least a bachelor's degree.

How well do immigrants speak English?

About half of immigrants ages 5 and older (52%) are proficient English speakers, meaning they either speak English very well or speak only English at home.

Again, there is a wide range of English proficiency depending on where immigrants were born:

- The overwhelming majority of immigrants from elsewhere in North America (97%) or from Oceania (83%) – primarily Australia and New Zealand – are proficient English speakers.
- Large shares of immigrants from sub-Saharan Africa (75%), South Asia (72%) and Europe (72%) also are English proficient.
- On the opposite end of the spectrum, only about one-in-three immigrants who were born in Central America (31%) are proficient in English.

English proficiency is more common among immigrants who arrived in the U.S. before 2000 than among those who entered the country later. Some 57% of immigrants who came to the U.S. before 2000 are proficient English speakers, compared with 47% who arrived in 2010 or later.

Note: This is an update of an analysis originally published May 3, 2017.

Facts About Unauthorized Immigrants

The number of unauthorized immigrants living in the United States has dropped to the level it was in 2004, and Mexicans are no longer a majority of this population. This decline is due mainly to a large drop in the number of new unauthorized immigrants, especially Mexicans, coming into the country. The origin countries of unauthorized immigrants also shifted during that time, with the number from Mexico declining and the number rising from Central America and Asia, according to the latest Pew Research Center estimates.

Here are five facts about the unauthorized immigrant population in the U.S.

1. There were 10.5 million unauthorized immigrants in the U.S. in 2017, representing 3.2% of the total U.S. population that year. The 2017 unauthorized immigrant total is a 14% drop from the peak of 12.2 million in 2007, when this group was 4% of the U.S. population.

2. The number of Mexican unauthorized immigrants declined since 2007, while the total from other nations ticked up. Mexicans made up less than half of all unauthorized U.S. immigrants (47%) in 2017 for the first time, according to the Center's estimate, compared with 57% in 2007. Their numbers (and share of the total) have been declining in recent years: There were 4.9 million Mexican unauthorized immigrants living in the U.S. in 2017, down from 6.9 million in 2007.

Meanwhile, the total from other nations, 5.5 million in 2017, ticked up from 2007, when it was 5.3 million. The number of unauthorized immigrants has grown since 2007 from both Central America and Asia. There were 1.5 million Central American unauthorized immigrants in 2007 and 1.9 million in 2017. This growth was fueled mainly by immigrants from the Northern Triangle nations of El Salvador, Guatemala and Honduras. The number from Asia, 1.3 million in 2007, rose to 1.5 million in 2017.

At the same time, the number of unauthorized immigrants from South America and Europe decreased between 2007 and 2017. Other large regions (the Caribbean, Middle East-North Africa, sub-Saharan Africa and the rest of the world) did not change significantly during that time.

3. The U.S. civilian workforce includes 7.6 million unauthorized immigrants, representing a decline since 2007. Between 2007 and 2017, the number of unauthorized immigrant workers fell by 625,000, as did their share of the total U.S. workforce over the same period. In 2017, this group accounted for 4.6% of those in the U.S. who were working or were unemployed and looking for work.

4. Six states account for 57% of unauthorized immigrants: California, Texas, Florida, New York, New Jersey and Illinois. From 2007 to 2017, individual states experienced different trends. The unauthorized immigrant population decreased in a dozen states: Arizona, California, Colorado, Florida, Georgia, Illinois, Michigan, Nevada, New Jersey, New Mexico, New York and Oregon. In five states, the unauthorized immigrant population rose over the same period: Louisiana, Maryland, Massachusetts, North Dakota and South Dakota.

5. A rising share of unauthorized immigrants have lived in the U.S. for more than a decade. About two-thirds (66%) of unauthorized immigrant adults in 2017 had been in the U.S. more than 10 years, compared with 41% in 2007. A declining share of unauthorized immigrants have lived in the U.S. for five years or less – 20% of adults in 2017, compared with 30% in 2007. In 2017, unauthorized immigrant adults had lived in the U.S. for a median of 15.1 years, meaning that half had been in the country at least that long.

"5 facts about illegal immigration in the U.S." by Jens Manuel Krogstad, Jeffrey S. Passel and D'Vera Cohn, Pew Research Center, June 12, 2019.

Viewpoint 3

> "...*individuals who arrive in the United States legally and overstay their visas comprise a significant portion of the undocumented population.*"

U.S. Immigration Policy Is Constantly Changing

Diane Roy, Claire Klobucista, and Amelia Cheatham

In the following viewpoint, Diane Roy, Claire Klobucista, and Amelia Cheatham discuss how the U.S. Congress has struggled to comprehensively reform immigration policy and law in the United States, causing U.S. presidents to turn to executive actions in order to reshape asylum and border policies. They delve into how this has resulted in a yo-yo effect, with each president reversing the policies of his predecessor and implementing his own in response to the influx of migrants seeking to live in America. This article was written in 2024, so it ends its analysis with the Biden administration's policies.

As you read, consider the following questions:

1. What do the authors suggest are the main reasons Congress has been unable to effectively reform U.S. immigration policy and law?

"The U.S. Immigration Debate" by Diana Roy, Claire Klobucista and Amelia Cheatham, Council on Foreign Relations, August 7, 2024.From CFR.org. Reprinted with permission. For more analysis on immigration and foreign policy, visit CFR.org.

2. As opposed to government officials, how do most everyday Americans feel about immigration, and how has this contributed to the overall debate surrounding immigration policy?
3. How has the response of state and local governments to the issue been different from the response at the federal level, and how has this impacted the overall ability of the U.S. government to find a comprehensive solution?

Immigration has been a touchstone of the U.S. political debate for decades, as policymakers have weighed economic, security, and humanitarian concerns. However, Congress has continued to disagree on comprehensive immigration reform, effectively moving some major policy decisions into the executive and judicial branches of government and fueling debate in the halls of state and municipal governments.

Former President Donald Trump has put efforts to reshape asylum, border, and deportation policy at the center of his political movement. President Joe Biden had pledged to reverse Trump's first-term actions and reform the system, but the end of pandemic-related border restrictions and a historic surge in migration have complicated his plans.

What is the immigrant population in the United States?

Immigrants composed an estimated 13.9 percent of the U.S. population in 2022, amounting to roughly 46 million people out of a total of almost 335 million, according to U.S. Census Bureau data released in April 2024. Together, immigrants and their U.S.-born children made up about 27 percent of U.S. inhabitants, per the Current Population Survey. Though the share of the population that is foreign born has steadily risen since 1970, when there were fewer than ten million immigrants in the country, recent figures still fall below the record high of 14.8 percent in 1890.

As of 2022, Mexico was the top country of origin for U.S. immigrants, with Mexicans constituting 23 percent of the total immigrant population. Other major countries of origin include India (6 percent); China, including Hong Kong and Macau (5 percent); and the Philippines (4 percent).

Undocumented immigration.

The U.S. government estimated the undocumented population to be some eleven million people in 2022. This total represents a slight decrease from 11.8 million before the 2008 economic crisis, which led some immigrants to return to their home countries and discouraged others from coming to the United States. In fiscal year 2023 (FY 2023), Customs and Border Protection (CBP) apprehended nearly 2.5 million people trying to illegally cross the southern U.S. border, a record high.

Until 2013, almost all of those trying to cross the U.S.-Mexico border were Mexican citizens, and most were individuals seeking work. Between 2013 and 2021, most immigrants came from Asia, particularly China and India. Mexico has since regained its status as the top country of origin, and Central Americans have made up an increasingly larger share of migrants at the southern U.S. border. Generally, they are coming not for work but to make asylum claims, and many of them are unaccompanied children. Some of these immigrants have different legal rights from Mexican nationals in the United States: Under a 2008 anti–human trafficking law, unaccompanied minors from noncontiguous countries have a right to a hearing before being deported to their home countries. The increase in Central American migration has strained the U.S. immigration system. At the end of FY 2023, there were nearly 2.8 million cases pending in immigration courts, the most on record.

Though many of the policies that aim to reduce unlawful immigration focus on enforcement at the border, individuals who arrive in the United States legally and overstay their visas comprise a significant portion of the undocumented population. A Center for Migration Studies report found that, between 2010 and 2018, individuals who overstayed their visas far outnumbered those who arrived by crossing the border illegally.

Legal immigration.

The United States granted more than one million individuals legal permanent residency in FY 2022, close to pre-pandemic levels. Some 58 percent of them were admitted on the basis of family reunification. Other categories included: employment-based preferences (27 percent), refugees (3 percent), diversity (4 percent), and asylees (5 percent). As of late 2023, more than four million applicants were on the State Department's waiting list for family- and employer-related immigrant visas, nearly a third of whom were from Mexico.

Hundreds of thousands of foreign nationals work legally in the United States under various types of nonimmigrant visas. In FY 2023, the United States granted more than 265,000 visas for high-skilled workers, known as H1B visas, and over 310,000 visas for temporary workers in agriculture and other industries, or H2A visas. H1B visas are capped at 85,000 per fiscal year, with exceptions for certain fields.

Immigrants made up 18.6 percent of the U.S. civilian workforce in 2023, according to the Bureau of Labor Statistics, up from 18.1 percent the previous year. Compared to those born in the United States, greater shares of immigrants worked in service fields (21.8 percent of all foreign-born people); production, transportation, and material moving (15.2 percent); and natural resources, construction, and maintenance (13.8 percent).

How do Americans feel about immigration?

A February 2024 poll by Gallup showed that 28 percent of surveyed Americans considered immigration to be the top problem facing the United States. In a separate Gallup poll conducted that same month, the majority of respondents felt that illegal immigration was a "critical" threat to U.S. national security.

A Pew Research Center poll conducted in April found that some 60 percent of the registered voters surveyed believed that undocumented immigrants currently in the United States should be allowed to stay, with 36 percent of respondents saying that undocumented immigrants should have the opportunity to apply for citizenship. In addition, a large majority of Americans still consider immigration to be overall good for the country.

How has Congress tried to address the issue?

The most recent push for an immigration policy overhaul was in 2013, following a decade in which Congress debated numerous immigration reforms, some considered comprehensive and others piecemeal. (Comprehensive immigration reform refers to omnibus legislation that attempts to address the following issues: demand for high- and low-skilled labor, the legal status of the millions of undocumented immigrants living in the country, border security, and interior enforcement.) The last major legislation to make it through Congress was under President Ronald Reagan in 1986, when his administration granted legal amnesty to some three million undocumented residents; in 1990, President George H.W. Bush further expanded legal immigration by increasing the cap for immigrant visas from 270,000 to 700,000, though he lowered the quota to 675,000 after several years. In 2007, President George W. Bush worked with congressional Democrats to reach a compromise on a new comprehensive bill, but it ultimately failed to win enough support in the Senate.

President Barack Obama pressed hard for a comprehensive bill that would pair a path to legalization for undocumented residents with stronger border security provisions. The Democrat-led Senate passed this legislation in 2013, but the bill stalled in the Republican-controlled House of Representatives. Both Presidents Trump and Biden put forward their own plans, which were not seriously considered by Congress.

What was the Obama administration's approach?

With legislation thwarted, Obama focused on executive action, a tactic that his successors continued. In 2012, his administration began a program known as DACA, or Deferred Action for Childhood Arrivals, which offered renewable, two-year deportation deferrals and work permits to undocumented immigrants who had arrived in the United States as children and had no criminal records.

Obama characterized the move as a "stopgap measure" and urged Congress to pass the DREAM Act, or Development Relief and Education for Alien Minors—legislation first introduced in 2001 that would have benefited many of the same people. Since then, more than 830,000 people have participated in DACA, and it's estimated that almost 1.2 million more were eligible as of 2023. Obama attempted to extend similar benefits to undocumented parents of U.S. citizens and permanent residents through a program known as Deferred Action for Parents of Americans (DAPA), but the Supreme Court effectively killed it in 2016.

In 2014, Obama also grappled with a surge of more than sixty thousand unaccompanied minors at the southern border, mostly from Central America. He directed $750 million in aid to the region to improve conditions there. Meanwhile, his administration faced criticism for its enforcement policies, including detaining children in poor conditions and overseeing the deportation of more people—approximately three million—than either the Bill Clinton or George W. Bush administrations had.

What was the Trump administration's approach?

Immigration remains a signature issue for Trump. He blames previous administrations for failing to secure the southern border, and in his first term, he advocated for sharply reducing both legal and illegal immigration. He repeatedly used executive action to reshape asylum, deportation, and border policy.

Border security and enforcement.

Trump vowed to expand the wall along the U.S.-Mexico border, which he claimed would stop drugs and gangs from entering the country. He was unsuccessful in securing funding from Congress, leading to a federal government shutdown in 2019 and a subsequent declaration of a national emergency, which allowed him to divert funds to build the wall.

Other enforcement measures under Trump included increasing border personnel; sending thousands of active-duty troops to the border; threatening Mexico with tariffs if it did not increase its own border enforcement; and attempting to cut federal funding to so-called sanctuary cities, or jurisdictions that refuse to enforce federal immigration directives.

Trump also ratcheted up previous administrations' deterrence efforts. He implemented a zero-tolerance policy, under which authorities arrested and prosecuted everyone caught crossing the southern border without authorization. This caused thousands of family separations, since by law children must be held apart from parents facing criminal prosecution. (Presidents Bush and Obama likewise faced criticism for child detention, but they did not make separations a matter of policy.)

DACA.

Trump sought to end DACA, calling it unconstitutional. The move spurred multiple legal challenges and, in June 2020, the Supreme Court blocked Trump's plan. A December 2020 federal court ruling forced the Trump administration to resume accepting new applicants.

Travel bans and refugee cap.

Trump aimed to sharply reduce the number of refugees and other immigrants granted legal entry into the United States. In 2017, he instituted a ban on immigration and travel from several Muslim-majority countries, including Iran, Somalia, and Yemen. The original order was rejected by the courts, but the Supreme Court upheld a more limited version. Trump also lowered the cap on the number of refugees the United States accepts each year to less than fifteen thousand for FY 2021—the lowest figure in the history of the U.S. refugee program. Additionally, he ended temporary protected status (TPS)—a program that allows migrants from certain crisis-stricken nations to live and work in the United States for a limited period—for several countries.

Asylum policy.

Trump implemented new restrictions on asylum seekers. In 2018, the administration began "metering" asylum applications, or only accepting a limited number each day. The next year, it launched the Migrant Protection Protocols, also known as the "Remain in Mexico" program, which required asylum seekers to wait in Mexico while their cases were processed in U.S. courts. At the same time, it sought "safe third country" agreements with several Latin American countries, which would have allowed U.S. authorities to send asylum seekers who traveled through those countries back there. Only an agreement with Guatemala was implemented before that country terminated it in 2021. Additionally, the Trump administration invoked Title 42, previously a rarely used public health law, to deny asylum on health-related grounds amid the COVID-19 pandemic.

Comprehensive reform effort. Like his immediate predecessors, Trump proposed broad immigration reform. His would have created a merit-based system to replace the current one, which prioritizes family reunification. It also included an expansion of the border wall and an employment verification system known as E-Verify, but it did not address the status of current undocumented residents. Congress ultimately did not take up the proposal.

What has been Biden's approach?

Ahead of the 2020 presidential election, Biden campaigned on overturning almost all of Trump's immigration policies. Since then, the Biden administration has reduced immigration enforcement within the United States, ended the travel bans, expanded green-card access for certain undocumented immigrants, and ended the controversial Title 42 policy, though it did initially maintain many pandemic-related restrictions. The administration also initially halted construction of the U.S.-Mexico border wall, though it has since moved forward with plans to build additional sections; expanded TPS protections; terminated the Remain in Mexico program (with Supreme Court approval); and raised the refugee cap to 125,000 for fiscal years 2022–24.

However, Biden's efforts to undo Trump-era policies have been challenged by a historic influx of migrants at the southern border. The record surge in border crossings has prompted the administration to implement several new restrictions since 2023, including a so-called transit ban allowing the government to deny asylum to migrants who did not previously apply for protection in a third country. In addition, the administration can temporarily bar asylum requests when the number of illegal crossings exceeds a certain threshold; since the start of 2024, illegal crossings have slowed.

Meanwhile, Biden has worked with Latin American leaders to increase aid to refugee populations, improve border management, and better coordinate emergency responses, even as his own comprehensive immigration reform bill and other border security legislation have failed in Congress. His administration has also launched efforts to accelerate the reunification of migrant families, including by reinstating the Central American Minors (CAM) program, which reunites children in the so-called Northern Triangle countries with their parents in the United States, and by creating a family-reunification task force. Additionally, Biden has pledged to invest $4 billion to address the drivers of migration from Central America, and he has sought to revive DACA; the Department of Homeland Security continues to accept and process renewal requests amid ongoing legal challenges to the program.

How are state and local authorities handling these issues?

States vary widely in how they treat unauthorized immigrants. Some, including California and Massachusetts, allow undocumented immigrants to apply for drivers' licenses, receive in-state tuition at universities, and obtain other benefits. At the other end of the spectrum are states such as Texas, where the legislature passed a law mandating that local governments and law enforcement agencies cooperate with federal immigration officers.

The federal government is generally responsible for enforcing immigration laws, but it delegates some immigration-related duties to state and local law enforcement. However, the degree to which local officials are obliged to cooperate with federal authorities is a subject of intense debate: dozens of counties across thirteen states are home to so-called sanctuary cities that limit cooperation with immigration enforcement. The degree to which local officials are obliged to cooperate with federal authorities is a subject of intense debate.

President Trump decried these sanctuary jurisdictions and reinstated a controversial Obama-era program known as Secure Communities, in which the FBI shares fingerprints of suspects collected by state and local law enforcement with federal immigration authorities. Under the program, state and local agencies also hand over individuals presumed to be in the country illegally. Biden terminated the program shortly after taking office.

A range of court rulings during the Trump era increased pressure on states. In 2018, the Justice Department launched a lawsuit against California over sanctuary jurisdictions, which was ultimately dismissed by the Supreme Court. It filed similar suits against New Jersey and Washington, and a federal court ruled in 2020 that the Trump administration could withhold federal funding from sanctuary jurisdictions, including New York City. Under Biden, the Justice Department reversed this stance, leading the Supreme Court to dismiss several pending cases.

The ongoing border crisis has driven increasing controversy over local responses. After Trump called on states to deploy National Guard contingents to the southern border, several governors refused. Others, including Texas's Greg Abbott, embraced Trump's views, continuing to expand the border wall and seeking to boost the role of state and local law enforcement in carrying out federal immigration policy. In the Biden era, Abbott has sought to impose stronger enforcement at the Texas-Mexico border despite federal opposition. The governor signed a law in December 2023 making it a state crime to cross the border into Texas illegally and authorizing law enforcement to arrest and deport migrants. The bill remains on hold amid legal challenges; several other states are attempting to enact similar legislation.

Viewpoint 4

> *"New arrivals can't simply be added to the existing estimate because some unauthorized immigrants leave the country every year, some die and some gain lawful status."*

Facts and Figures About Unauthorized Immigrants Are Not Always Accurate

Jeffrey S. Passel and Jens Manuel Krogstad

In the following report from the Pew Research Center, Jeffrey S. Passel and Jens Manuel Krogstad present and discuss recent statistics specifically regarding undocumented, or unauthorized, immigrants in the United States. They also address some of the issues surrounding gathering this data and several commonly held misconceptions about undocumented immigrants and their impact on the U.S. culture and economy.

As you read, consider the following questions:

1. What factors do the authors suggest are impacting the reliability of current statistics regarding undocumented immigrants in the United States?
2. Do the authors appear to be taking a particular stance or reflecting a particular bias regarding this issue?

"What we know about unauthorized immigrants living in the U.S." Pew Research Center, Washington, D.C. (July 22, 2024)

3. According to the article, which states have been most heavily impacted by undocumented immigrants? Why do you think this is the case?

The unauthorized immigrant population in the United States grew to 11.0 million in 2022, according to new Pew Research Center estimates based on the 2022 American Community Survey, the most recent year available. The increase from 10.5 million in 2021 reversed a long-term downward trend from 2007 to 2019. This is the first sustained increase in the unauthorized immigrant population since the period from 2005 to 2007.

However, the number of unauthorized immigrants living in the U.S. in 2022 was still below the peak of 12.2 million in 2007.

These new estimates do not reflect events since mid-2022. The U.S. unauthorized immigrant population has likely grown over the past two years, based on several alternative data sources. For example, encounters with migrants at U.S. borders reached record levels throughout 2022-23, and the number of applicants waiting for decisions on asylum claims increased by about 1 million by the end of 2023.

In addition, through December 2023, about 500,000 new immigrants were paroled into the country through two federal programs – the Cuban, Haitian, Nicaraguan and Venezuelan (CHNV) program and Uniting for Ukraine (U4U). Groups like these have traditionally been considered part of the unauthorized immigrant population, but almost none of them appear in the 2022 estimates.

While these new arrivals probably increased the U.S. unauthorized immigrant population, it remains to be seen how much. New arrivals can't simply be added to the existing estimate because some unauthorized immigrants leave the country every year, some die and some gain lawful status. (For details, read "What has happened with unauthorized migration since July 2022?")

What has happened with unauthorized migration since July 2022?

Here are key findings about how the U.S. unauthorized immigrant population changed recently:

- **The number of unauthorized immigrants from Mexico dropped to 4.0 million in 2022 from a peak of 6.9 million in 2007.** Mexico has long been, and remains, the most common country of birth for unauthorized immigrants.
- From 2019 to 2022, the unauthorized immigrant population from nearly every region of the world grew. The Caribbean, South America, Asia, Europe and sub-Saharan Africa all saw increases.
- **The unauthorized immigrant population grew in six states** from 2019 to 2022 – Florida, Maryland, Massachusetts, New Jersey, New York and Texas. Only California saw a decrease.
- **About 8.3 million U.S. workers in 2022 were unauthorized immigrants,** an increase from 7.4 million in 2019. The 2022 number is essentially the same as previous highs in 2008 and 2011.

Composition of the U.S. immigrant population

Immigrants made up 14.3% of the nation's population in 2022. That share was slightly higher than in the previous five years but below the record high of 14.8% in 1890.

As of 2022, **unauthorized immigrants represented 3.3% of the total U.S. population and 23% of the foreign-born population.** These shares were lower than the peak values in 2007 but slightly higher than in 2019.

Meanwhile, the *lawful* immigrant population grew steadily from 24.1 million in 2000 to 36.9 million in 2022. The growth was driven by a rapid increase in the number of naturalized citizens, from 10.7 million to 23.4 million. The number of lawful permanent residents dropped slightly, from 11.9 million to 11.5 million. As a result, in 2022, 49% of all immigrants in the country were naturalized U.S. citizens.

Who lives with unauthorized immigrants?

Unauthorized immigrants live in 6.3 million households that include more than 22 million people. These households represent 4.8% of the 130 million U.S. households.

Here are some facts about these households in 2022:

- In 86% of these households, either the householder or their spouse is an unauthorized immigrant.
- Almost 70% of these households are considered "mixed status," meaning that they also contain lawful immigrants or U.S.-born residents.
- In only about 5% of these households, the unauthorized immigrants are not related to the householder or spouse. In these cases, they are probably employees or roommates.

Of the 22 million people in households with an unauthorized immigrant, 11 million are U.S. born or lawful immigrants. They include:

- 1.3 million U.S.-born adults who are children of unauthorized immigrants. (We cannot estimate the total number of U.S.-born adult children of unauthorized immigrants because available data sources only identify those who still live with their unauthorized immigrant parents.)
- 1.4 million other U.S.-born adults and 3.0 million lawful immigrant adults.

About 4.4 million U.S.-born children under 18 live with an unauthorized immigrant parent. They account for about 84% of all minor children living with their unauthorized immigrant parent.

Altogether, about 850,000 children under 18 are unauthorized immigrants in 2022.

The share of households that include an unauthorized immigrant varies across states. In Maine, Mississippi, Montana and West Virginia, fewer than 1% of households include an unauthorized immigrant. Nevada (9%) has the highest share, followed by California, New Jersey and Texas (8% each).

What countries do unauthorized immigrants come from?

The origin countries for unauthorized immigrants have changed since the population peaked in 2007. Here are some highlights of those changes:

Mexico

The 4.0 million unauthorized immigrants from Mexico living in the U.S. in 2022 was the lowest number since the 1990s. And in 2022, Mexico accounted for 37% of the nation's unauthorized immigrants, by far the smallest share on record.

The decrease in unauthorized immigrants from Mexico reflects several factors:

- A broader decline in migration from Mexico to the U.S.;
- Some Mexican immigrants returning to Mexico; and
- Expanded opportunities for lawful immigration from Mexico and other countries, especially for temporary agricultural workers.

The rest of the world

The total number of unauthorized immigrants in the U.S. from countries other than Mexico grew rapidly between 2019 and 2022, from 5.8 million to 6.9 million.

The number of unauthorized immigrants from almost every world region increased. The largest increases were from the Caribbean (300,000) and Europe and Canada (275,000). One exception was Central America, which had led in growth until 2019 but saw no change after that.

After Mexico, the countries with the largest unauthorized immigrant populations in the U.S. in 2022 were:

- El Salvador (750,000)
- India (725,000)
- Guatemala (675,000)
- Honduras (525,000)

The Northern Triangle

Three Central American countries – El Salvador, Honduras and Guatemala – together represented 1.9 million unauthorized immigrants in the U.S. in 2022, or about 18% of the total. The unauthorized immigrant population from the Northern Triangle grew by about 50% between 2007 and 2019 but did not increase significantly after that.

Other origin countries

In 2022, Venezuela was the country of birth for 270,000 U.S. unauthorized immigrants. This population had seen particularly fast growth, from 55,000 in 2007 to 130,000 in 2017. It is poised to grow significantly in the future as new methods of entry to the U.S. are now available to Venezuelans.

Other countries with large numbers of unauthorized immigrants have also seen increases in recent years. Brazil, Canada, Colombia, Ecuador, India, and countries making up the former Soviet Union all experienced growth from 2019 to 2022.

However, other countries with significant unauthorized immigrant populations showed no change, notably China, the Dominican Republic and the Philippines.

Which states do unauthorized immigrants call home?

Most U.S. states' unauthorized immigrant populations stayed steady from 2019 to 2022. However, six states showed significant growth:

- Florida (+400,000)
- Texas (+85,000)
- New York (+70,000)
- New Jersey (+55,000)
- Massachusetts (+50,000)
- Maryland (+40,000)

California (-120,000) is the only state whose unauthorized immigrant population decreased.

States with the most unauthorized immigrants

The six states with the largest unauthorized immigrant populations in 2022 were:

- California (1.8 million)
- Texas (1.6 million)
- Florida (1.2 million)
- New York (650,000)
- New Jersey (475,000)
- Illinois (400,000)

These states have consistently had the most unauthorized immigrants since at least 1980. However, in 2007, California had *1.2 million more* unauthorized immigrants than Texas. Today, with the declining number in California, it has only about 150,000 more. The unauthorized immigrant population has also become considerably less geographically concentrated over time. In 2022, the top six states were home to 56% of the nation's unauthorized immigrants, down from 80% in 1990.

Unauthorized immigrants in the labor force

The number of unauthorized immigrants in the U.S. workforce grew from 7.4 million in 2019 to 8.3 million in 2022. The 2022 number equals previous highs in 2008 and 2011.

Unauthorized immigrants represent about 4.8% of the U.S. workforce in 2022. This was below the peak of 5.4% in 2007.

Since 2003, unauthorized immigrants have made up 4.4% to 5.4% of all U.S. workers, a relatively narrow range.

The share of the U.S. workforce made up by unauthorized immigrants is higher than their 3.3% share of the total U.S. population. That's because the unauthorized immigrant population includes relatively few children or elderly adults, groups that tend not to be in the labor force.

The share of unauthorized immigrants in the workforce varied across states in 2022. Nevada (9%), Texas (8%), Florida (8%), New Jersey (7%), California (7%) and Maryland (7%) had the highest shares, while fewer than 1% of workers in Maine, Montana, Vermont and West Virginia were unauthorized immigrants.

Note: This is an update of a post originally published Nov. 16, 2023.

Periodical and Internet Sources Bibliography

The following articles have been selected to supplement the diverse views presented in this chapter.

Edward Alden, "Biden's New Southern Border Plan Might Just Work," Council on Foreign Relations, April 12, 2023. https://www.cfr.org/article/bidens-new-southern-border-plan-might-just-work.

Muzaffar Chishti, Kathleen Bush-Joseph, and Colleen Putzel-Kavanaugh, "Biden at the Three-Year Mark: The Most Active Immigration Presidency Yet is Mired in Border Crisis Narrative", Migration Policy Institute, January 19, 2024. https://www.migrationpolicy.org/article/biden-three-immigration-record.

Dara Lind, "The Crisis at the U.S. Southern Border", The President's Inbox, March 12, 2024. https://www.cfr.org/podcasts/crisis-us-southern-border-dara-lind.

Migration Data Hub, N.d., "U.S. Annual Refugee Resettlement Ceilings and Number of Refugees Admitted, 1980-Present," Migration Policy Institute, January 10, 2024. https://www.migrationpolicy.org/programs/data-hub/charts/us-refugee-resettlement.

Jeffrey Passel & Jens Krogstad, "U.S. Unauthorized Immigrant Population Reached a Record 14 Million in 2023," Pew Research Center, August 21, 2025. https://www.pewresearch.org/race-and-ethnicity/2025/08/21/u-s-unauthorized-immigrant-population-reached-a-record-14-million-in-2023/.

Eduardo Porter and Youyou Zhou, "How America tried and failed to stay White," *The Washington Post,* May 15, 2024. https://www.washingtonpost.com/opinions/interactive/2024/immigration-history-race-quota-progress/.

"Refugee Admissions Report," U.S. State Department, Bureau of Population, Refugees, and Migration, Refugee Processing Center, January 5, 2024. https://www.wrapsnet.org/admissions-and-arrivals/.

Diana Roy, Amelia Cheatham, and Claire Klobucista, "How the U.S. Patrols Its Borders," Council on Foreign Relations, July 28, 2025. https://www.cfr.org/backgrounder/how-us-patrols-its-borders.

"U.S. Postwar Immigration Policy," Council on Foreign Relations, 1952-2025. https://www.cfr.org/timeline/us-postwar-immigration-policy.

Jill H. Wilson, "Temporary Protected Status and Deferred Enforced Departure," Congressional Research Service, Washington, D.C., August 28, 2025. https://www.congress.gov/crs-product/RS20844.

Chapter 2

Is Immigration Detrimental to the United States?

Chapter Preface

One of the biggest topics of debate surrounding U.S. immigration policy is whether or not immigrants are helpful or detrimental to the country as a whole.

Those on one side of the debate sometimes argue that immigrants, documented or undocumented, take on the jobs that other Americans don't want. Therefore, they boost the country's economy.

The other side argues that immigrants are responsible for a lot of crime and use state and federal assistance programs, which results in higher costs for citizens.

The viewpoints in this chapter present statistics and opinions related to both sides of this argument. The main viewpoints presented explore this issue from mostly economic and criminal standpoints. Sidebars address perceived misconceptions about statistics in these same areas.

The views presented in this chapter have helped inform U.S. immigration policy in the past, continue to influence U.S. immigration policy in the present, and will help determine U.S. immigration policies far into the future.

Viewpoint 1

> *"The reality is that the economy does not have a fixed number of jobs, and what we see today is a growing economy that is adding jobs for both immigrants and U.S.-born workers."*

Immigrants Are Not Hurting U.S.-Born Workers

Daniel Costa and Heidi Shierholz

In this viewpoint, Daniel Costa and Heidi Shierholz present recent statistics about job distribution between U.S.-born and immigrant workers to combat claims that immigrants are taking employment away from U.S. citizens. They argue that the problems workers face stem from weak policies governing the labor force and other dynamics placing too much power with corporations and employers. They argue that the narrative that immigrants are taking jobs from U.S. citizens does not reflect the reality workers are experiencing.

As you read, consider the following questions:

1. What sources of information do the authors cite in their argument, and are these sources independent and reliable?
2. What do the authors suggest is the real purpose behind the narrative that immigrants are taking jobs from U.S. citizens, and does this motivation detract from the claim?

3. What effect would the changes suggested by the authors have for both immigrants and U.S. citizens?

The immigrant share of the labor force reached a record high of 18.6% in 2023, according to our analysis of Current Population Survey (CPS) data from the Bureau of Labor Statistics.1 Anti-immigration advocates have been out in full force, using this as a talking point for deeply misguided commentary and analysis that roughly translates to "immigrants are taking all our jobs."

The reality is that the economy does not have a fixed number of jobs, and what we see today is a growing economy that is adding jobs for both immigrants and U.S.-born workers. Here are six key facts that show immigrants are not hurting the employment outcomes of U.S.-born workers.

- **The unemployment rate for U.S.-born workers averaged 3.6% in 2023, the lowest rate on record.** Obviously, immigration is not causing high unemployment among U.S.-born workers.
- **The share of prime-age U.S.-born individuals with a job is at its highest rate in more than two decades.** In 2023, the prime-age (ages 25–54) employment-to-population ratio (EPOP) for U.S.-born individuals was 81.4%, up from 80.7% in 2019 and now at its highest rate since 2001.2, 3
- **The prime-age labor force participation rate (LFPR) for U.S.-born individuals is also at its highest rate in more than two decades.** In 2023, the LFPR for prime-age U.S.-born individuals was 83.9%, up from 83.3% in 2019 and now at its highest rate since 2002. Further, the increase in the U.S.-born prime-age LFPR over the last year was the second highest on record—below only the increase that occurred the year before last.4, 5
- **The prime-age LFPR of U.S.-born men without a bachelor's degree grew at a record pace in each of the last two years and is above its pre-COVID trend.** We focus here

on prime-age men without a bachelor's degree because though the immigrant population is comprised of men and women of all education levels, immigrants are somewhat disproportionately concentrated among men without a college degree (in 2023, the immigrant share of the overall labor force was 18.6%, but it was 20.0% of men without a college degree). That means that if recent immigration were affecting labor market outcomes of U.S.-born workers, it would be more easily detected among workers in this group. However, the LFPR of these workers is also beating expectations. *It is clear the labor market is both absorbing immigrants and generating strong job opportunities for U.S.-born workers, including those in demographic groups potentially most impacted by immigration. [See Notes 6, 7]*

- **Though the immigrant *share*** of the labor force reached a record high in 2023, immigrant labor force ***growth*** is not occurring at an unprecedented rate. From 2019 to 2023, the immigrant labor force grew 2.3% annually on average, according to our analysis of CPS data. That is strong growth, but it's roughly one-third the rate the economy experienced between 1996 and 2000 (which, just like 2022 and 2023, was a period of very low unemployment—and strong employment growth—for U.S.-born workers). Immigrant inflows into the labor force over the last year alone were also not unprecedentedly high—for example, the pace was slower than in 2022 and slower than three of the years from 1996–2000.
- **Immigrants are an integral part of our labor market, filling gaps caused by demographic changes in the United States and contributing to strong economic growth.** The immigrants that make up 18.6% of the U.S. labor force are playing key roles in numerous industries and are employed in a mix of lower, middle, and higher-wage jobs. And as the Congressional Budget Office recently reported, immigration is contributing to strong economic growth—with future

> immigration forecasted to boost real gross domestic product by 2% over the next 10 years—as well as increasing government revenue. Immigrants are also complementing U.S.-born workers by contributing to overall population and workforce growth. The U.S. Census Bureau projects that if the U.S. were to have lower-than-expected immigration levels, the population would begin to decline in 20 years, and if there were suddenly zero immigration, the population would begin to decline next year, deeply harming economic growth.

As these six facts show, the idea that immigrants are making things worse for U.S.-born workers is wrong. The reality is that the labor market is absorbing immigrants at a rapid pace, while simultaneously maintaining record-low unemployment for U.S.-born workers.

Claiming that immigrants are making things worse for U.S.-born workers is often used as an intentional distraction from dynamics that are actually hurting working people—such as weak labor standards and enforcement, anti-worker deregulation, weak labor law that fails to protect workers' rights to unions and collective bargaining in the face of coordinated and well-funded attacks, and other dynamics that result in too much power in the hands of corporations and employers.

While there's no question that the immigration system desperately needs updating so that workers are adequately protected, it's important to remember that it is *employers* that underpay and exploit workers based on their immigration status—committing workplace violations against those who lack status at a vastly higher rate than U.S.-born workers. And it is employers that regularly and even systematically steal wages from workers who only have a temporary, precarious status provided by a work visa. The resulting two-tiered system of rights in the workplace prevents immigrants from asserting and enforcing their rights. Reform efforts in Congress and the executive branch should thus focus on providing status and work authorization to those who lack it and compelling employers to follow the law, rather than more funding for, and draconian measures on, border enforcement, deportations, and detaining immigrants.

If those who mischaracterize immigration as bad for the economy and for U.S.-born workers really care about improving wages and working conditions for U.S.-born workers, they should focus on pushing for labor law reform and strong labor standards and helping ensure that all workers—regardless of immigration status—have equal and enforceable rights in the workplace.

Notes

Some data notes: We use full-year CPS data throughout this piece because breakdowns by immigration status aren't available on a seasonally adjusted basis. Also, breakdowns by immigration status are only available since 1994 in the CPS, so any time we talk about records in this piece, we mean since 1994.

While the overall U.S.-born EPOP grew substantially in each of the last three years, it is still below its pre-COVID level. However, the fact that it has not attained its pre-COVID level is not about immigration, it's largely about retiring baby boomers. Remember, the overall EPOP considers everyone age 16 and over, so when a large group of workers—like the baby boomers—hits retirement age, the EPOP "mechanically" drops. A common way to side-step this issue and to focus on trends that are actually related to the strength of job opportunities is to look only at so-called prime-age workers, workers ages 25–54, as we have done.

These findings hold if we restrict to data from the fourth quarter in every year. The prime-age EPOP of US-born workers was 81.6% in 2023Q4, up from 81.3% in 2019Q4 and now at its highest levels since 2000.

As with the EPOP, the overall LFPR for U.S.-born workers, though increasing at a record pace in the last two years, remains below its 2019 level—but again, that is not about immigration, it's about retiring baby boomers.

These findings hold if we restrict to data from the fourth quarter in every year. The prime-age LFPR of US-born people was 84.1% in 2023Q4, up from 83.8% in 2019Q4 and now at its highest level since 2002.

Details on the trend analysis: Due in large part to slack labor markets for much of the period (resulting from fiscal and monetary policy failures) and the erosion of job quality as a result of the dynamics mentioned in the conclusion of this piece, the LFPR of this group has been steadily declining in recent decades. Between the business cycle peaks of 2000 and 2019, the LFPR of this group declined from 89.4% to 84.9%, a decline of 0.24 percentage points per year, on average. If that trend had continued from 2019 to 2023, the LFPR of this group would have been 83.9% in 2023 instead of what it was, 84.5%. In other words, this group is beating expectations.

These findings hold if we restrict to data from the fourth quarter in every year. The prime-age LFPR of US-born men without a college degree has risen strongly in each of the last three years and is above its pre-COVID trend.]

> *"Immigration has an overall positive impact on the long-run economic growth in the U.S."*

Many Opinions About Immigrants and the Economy Are Myths

Gretchen Frazee

Below, Gretchen Frazee, a Senior Coordinating Broadcast Producer for the PBS NewsHour, presents counterpoints for four commonly-held beliefs about how immigrants are having a negative effect on the U.S. economy. She presents statistics and research in support of her claims and suggests other factors or organizations that should be held responsible instead of immigrants.

As you read, consider the following questions:

1. Is there an implicit bias in the author's argument, given the general policies and opinions of her employer and the general policies and politics of the administration she mentions in her article?
2. Why do first-generation immigrants cost the U.S. money up front, and how is the contrasting fiscal responsibility of second-generation immigrants important to the author's arguments?

"4 Myths About How Immigrants Affect the U.S. Economy," **by Gretchen Frazee, PBS NewsHour, November 2, 2018. Reprinted by permission.**

3. In what ways do immigrants complement and support U.S. workers, according to the author?

President Donald Trump has been stoking fears about immigrants in the days leading up to the midterm elections. He's tweeted anti-immigrant ads and threatened to revoke birthright citizenship, something lawmakers on both sides of the aisle have said would be unconstitutional, as he campaigns to drive up Republican turnout.

In a Thursday speech, Trump, a vocal critic of illegal immigration long before he reached the White House, claimed it costs the U.S. billions of dollars each year.

"Illegal immigration hurts Americans workers, burdens American taxpayers and undermines public safety, and places enormous strains on local schools, hospitals and communities in general, taking precious resources away from the poorest Americans who need them most," Trump said.

While Trump's rhetoric has lately focused on unauthorized immigrants, his policies have targeted legal immigration as well. Under his administration, refugee admissions in 2017 dropped to their lowest since at least 2002. Trump signed an executive order tightening restrictions on HB1 visas for skilled immigrants. He has pushed for a merit-based immigration system, and his administration has proposed cutting public benefits to legal immigrants.

Trump's characterization of immigrants, as people who drain public resources, however, is not backed by the data. Unauthorized immigrants aren't usually eligible for federal benefits, for instance, and multiple studies have found that immigrants help the economy grow.

Here are some of the most widespread myths about how immigrants affect the U.S. economy, and the research that refutes them.

Myth #1: Immigrants take more from the U.S. government than they contribute

Fact: Immigrants contribute more in tax revenue than they take in government benefits

A 2017 report from the National Academies of Sciences, Engineering, and Medicine found immigration "has an overall positive impact on the long-run economic growth in the U.S." How that breaks down is important.

First-generation immigrants cost the government more than native-born Americans, according to the report — about $1,600 per person annually. But second generation immigrants are "among the strongest fiscal and economic contributors in the U.S.," the report found. They contribute about $1,700 per person per year. All other native-born Americans, including third generation immigrants, contribute $1,300 per year on average.

It is difficult to determine the exact cost or contribution of unauthorized immigrants because they are harder to survey, but the study suggests they likely have a more positive effect than their legal counterparts because they are, on average, younger and do not qualify for public benefits.

It's also important to note that less-educated immigrants tend to work more than people with the same level of education born in the U.S. About half of all U.S.-born Americans with no high school diploma work, compared to about 70 percent of immigrants with the same education level, Giovanni Peri, an economics professor at the University of California, Davis, said in a recent interview with PBS NewsHour.

In general, more people working means more taxes — and that's true overall with undocumented immigrants as well. Undocumented immigrants pay an estimated $11.6 billion a year in taxes, according to the Institute on Taxation & Economic Policy.

Immigrants are also less likely to take public benefits than the native-born population for two reasons.

First, to receive most public benefits under the social safety net, immigrants must be lawful permanent residents for at least five years.

There are approximately 9 million immigrants that fit that definition in the U.S. Of those, many would not qualify for welfare or other programs because their incomes are too high.

"While it is really important to ensure that immigrants and their children have access to the safety net, there are already a lot of eligibility barriers in place," said Hamutal Bernstein, a senior research associate at the Urban Institute.

Many immigrants are hesitant to take public benefits even if they are eligible, Peri said.

"There is a little bit of a stigma in applying for welfare because they have come here to work, to support their families," Peri said.

Immigrants can be a financial burden to state and local governments through the cost of sending their children to public school — something Trump mentioned Thursday.

But Trump's claim ignored a critical point. Educating those children has economic benefits later down the road when they get better-paying jobs and, in turn, pay higher taxes.

Myth #2: Immigrants take American jobs

Fact: Immigrant workers often take jobs that boost other parts of the economy

Immigrants make up 17 percent of the U.S. labor force, according to the U.S. Bureau of Labor Statistics, but few experts believe they're taking jobs from Americans, as Trump claims.

"Most economists agree that in spite of being a very big part of the labor force, immigrants have not come at the cost either of American jobs, nor of American wages," Peri, the UC Davis professor, said.

The reason is that immigrants often have jobs that Americans tend not to take. So instead of competing with Americans' for work, immigrants tend to complement American workers.

On a farm, for example, owners, managers and salespeople are often born in America. Immigrants tend to work as field hands. Neither group could do their job without the other.

Immigrants who work as child care providers give Americans, specifically women, more opportunity to join the labor force. And immigrants are playing an increasingly critical role in taking care of the elderly as baby boomers retire. Census data shows that immigrants accounted for 24 percent of nursing, psychiatric and home care aides in 2015.

A study from the bipartisan research organization New American Economy found immigrants were 15 percent more likely to work unusual hours than similar U.S.-born workers. They are also more likely to be employed in dangerous jobs, according to data from the American Community Survey and Bureau of Statistics.

In addition, the latest jobs report shows the U.S. economy performing strongly enough that it can absorb large numbers of workers, including immigrants.

Immigrants fill those roles in part because they are on average less educated than native-born Americans. About 26 percent have less than a high school degree, compared to 5 percent of native-born workers, according to the Urban Institute. But one in three immigrant workers have a college or advanced degree, a rate on par with Americans born here. Unauthorized immigrants tend to have slightly lower education levels; about 13 percent have college degrees.

Myth #3: The U.S. economy does not need immigrants

Fact: Immigrants are key to offsetting a falling birth rate

The U.S. birth rate is 1.8 births per woman, down from 3.65 in 1960, according to the World Bank. Demographers consider 2.1 births per woman as the rate needed to replace the existing population.

According to the Pew Research Center, if not for immigrants, the U.S. workforce would be shrinking. That would create a host of problems for the federal government.

If not for immigrants, the U.S. workforce would be shrinking.

Social Security, which is paid for by current workers, would be in even more serious budgetary trouble than it already is. Economic growth would also likely stagnate or even contract, as it has in Japan, a country where the population is shrinking and does not attract many immigrants.

Automation can buttress economic growth for a while, but investment in new technology only goes so far, said Betsey Stevenson, an associate professor of economics at the University of Michigan.

Plus, immigrants increase demand for goods and services, which further boosts economic growth, she added.

Myth #4: It would be better for the economy if immigrants' children were not citizens

Fact: Children with citizenship are more productive workers

At his rally Thursday night in Columbia, Missouri, Trump criticized the 14th Amendment, which was ratified after the Civil War and guaranteed citizenship to "all persons born or naturalized in the United States," including people who were formerly enslaved.

Trump said the idea was "a crazy, lunatic policy" supported by Democrats that today allows "hundreds of thousands of children born to illegal immigrants" to become citizens each year.

Research shows that repealing birthright citizenship could have significant negative consequences for the U.S. economy because children who are citizens have more economic opportunity and rely less on government assistance.

A Migration Policy Institute analysis estimates the number of unauthorized immigrants would increase from 11 million to 16 million by 2050 if birthright citizenship were repealed.

"Over the course of decades, you'd end up with a growing population that is cut off from the rest of society because they live in fear of deportation and they can't get jobs," said Randy Capps, the director of research for U.S. programs at the Migration Policy Institute.

Take, for example, the population of so-called "Dreamers" who were brought to the U.S. illegally as children. One study estimated the U.S. is losing out on $15 billion in economic potential from that group because they often face problems getting into college and getting a job.

An experiment in Germany, which does not have birthright citizenship, also showed that when children of immigrants were given citizenship at birth, those children experienced better health outcomes and had fewer children of their own.

VIEWPOINT 3

> *"Typically, more criminal charges are listed on court documents for non-citizens who were admitted into the country lawfully compared to those who entered the country unlawfully."*

Immigrants Are Committing Fewer Crimes

Transactional Records Access Clearinghouse

Here, the Transactional Records Access Clearinghouse (TRAC) lays out data collected from multiple court and police records regarding the frequency with which both documented and undocumented immigrants are arrested, criminally charged, and deported due to those charges.

As you read, consider the following questions:

1. Are the sources of TRAC's information reliable? Why or why not?
2. What conclusions, if any, does TRAC draw from this data?
3. What types of supporting evidence are required for ICE attorneys in order to justify deportation? Does this level of evidence seem unduly strict or unreasonably lenient? Does it seem fair?

Over the past decade, the number of criminal-related charges listed on Notices to Appear as the basis for deportation has declined dramatically. In 2010, across all Notices to Appear (NTAs) received by the immigration courts that year, ICE listed a total of 57,199 criminal-related grounds for deportation. By 2021, just over a decade later, that number dropped to 8,694, less than a sixth of its original height.

Typically, more criminal charges are listed on court documents for non-citizens who were admitted into the country lawfully compared to those who entered the country unlawfully. For instance, in FY 2021, a total of 5,895 criminal-related charges were listed on NTAs for lawfully admitted immigrants compared to 2,799 for immigrants who were not lawfully admitted. See Figure 1 (and Table 1 below).

This trend emerges at the same time that Immigration and Customs Enforcement's (ICE) immigration enforcement activities throughout the United States have expanded dramatically through programs such as 287(g) and Secure Communities, and at the same time that questions about the relationship between immigration and crime have taken center stage in political discourse.

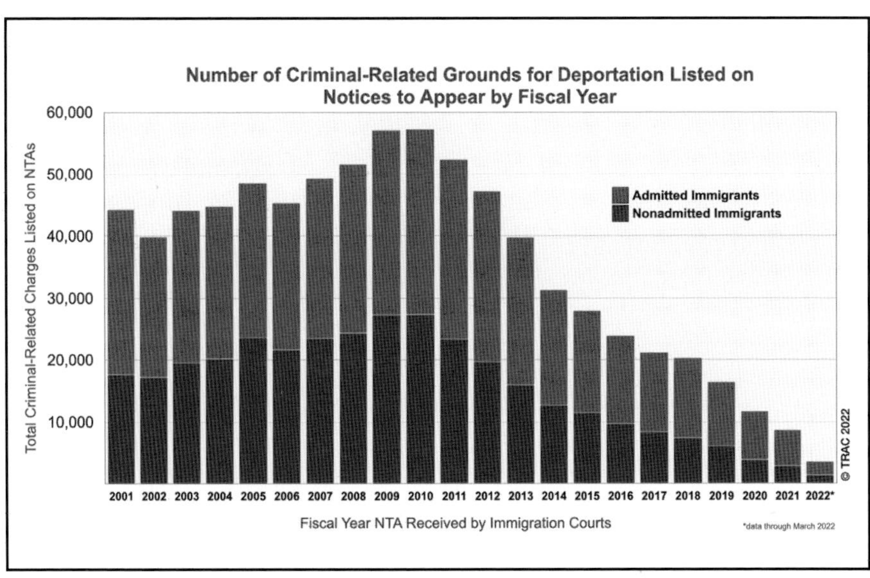

Criminal related grounds for deportation are not, in themselves, criminal charges, and deportation hearings are not trials to determine criminal guilt. In fact, some criminal grounds for deportation do not require an underlying criminal conviction at all. Moreover, non-citizens may have a criminal record that is not represented on an NTA. Nonetheless, due to the increasingly complex and overlapping relationship between the criminal justice system and the immigration enforcement systems—what some immigration experts have called "crimmigration"[1]—TRAC has begun tracking the volume and type of criminal-related charges listed on NTAs each year.

TRAC's new Criminal Grounds for Deportation table makes annual charge totals available starting in fiscal year 2017 and updates each month with current data. The charges listed represent all charges on all NTAs received by the court, not the number of cases. Individual cases may involve one or multiple criminal-related grounds for deportation. The underlying data for this table comes from case-by-case Immigration Court records which were obtained and analyzed by the Transactional Records Access Clearinghouse (TRAC) at Syracuse University through a series of Freedom of Information Act (FOIA) requests to the Executive Office for Immigration Review (EOIR).

Immigrants who are in the United States and who violate certain parts of the Immigration and Nationality Act may be deported through deportation proceedings in Immigration Court.[2]The Notice to Appear (NTA) is a charging document issued by agencies within the Department of Homeland Security to non-citizens that the agency believes should be deported. NTAs are then filed with the Immigration Courts, which marks the beginning of a deportation (or removal) proceeding. Deportation proceedings typically end with an Immigration Judge granting permission for the non-citizen to remain in the United State on a temporary or permanent basis, or issuing a deportation order.

In order to justify the assertion that an immigrant should be deported, ICE attorneys must provide one or more specific parts of US immigration law that an immigrant has violated. Based on data received from the Immigration Courts, TRAC identifies about 160 various charges. TRAC categorizes charges based on levels of seriousness, including terrorism charges, national security charges, aggravated felonies, criminal-related charges, immigration-specific charges, and those cases where only an unlawful entry is listed. Immigration-specific charges include charges of violating the terms of one's visa, using fraudulent immigration documents, or becoming a public charge.

The aggravated felony category was introduced in 1988 not as an independent criminal charge, but as a way of classifying certain criminal charges for immigration purposes only. If the government classifies a crime as an aggravated felony, it could mean that the individual has fewer options for remaining in the United States lawfully (such as barring individuals from applying for asylum) and may not be permitted to be released from immigrant detention. [3]

Other criminal-related grounds for deportation are specifically outlined in the Immigration and Nationality Act, and include charges for controlled substances, firearms offenses, domestic violence, or the "quite complex"[4] crimes involving moral turpitude.

Immigration law makes an important distinction between criminal-related grounds of deportation for immigrants who have been lawfully admitted[5] to the country and those who have not.[6] It is beyond the scope of this report to examine all of the differences, but generally immigrants who have not been lawfully admitted face fewer procedural protections and exceptions than immigrants who have been admitted lawfully. Conversely, in filing cases against immigrants who have been lawfully admitted, ICE may be more inclined to list criminal-related grounds since the agency would not usually have recourse, by definition, to charging unlawful entry.

There are important caveats to these data. NTAs are not a record of all criminal charges and convictions in a person's criminal history. For instance, an individual may have a charge or conviction in a local court, but those may not be included on the NTA. ICE attorneys have the discretion to choose which (if any) criminal-related grounds to include on an NTA, and a criminal charge is not a requirement for deportation. In fact, to limit the number of charges the agency needs to sustain in court, ICE may choose to only charge a non-citizen with an immigration-related charge (such as unlawful entry) in order to lessen the burden on the agency in court. Moreover, immigrants may come to ICE's attention based on routine local policing (i.e. a traffic stop) in which no charge or conviction ever took place. And not all criminal violations, even after a conviction, are a basis under immigration statutes for removal. Finally, these data do not show the final disposition of the allegations on an NTA, and therefore do not show whether ICE's charges were upheld, challenged, dropped, or revised by the end of the case.

With these caveats in mind, a few plausible (but not exhaustive) explanations emerge to answer the question implied by the steady decline in the use of criminal-related grounds for deportation listed on NTAs. The expansion of ICE's immigration enforcement network over the past 15 years may mean that local law enforcement agencies are less inclined to pursue criminal charges when they know that suspects are likely to be deported, leading to fewer criminal-related grounds of deportation. Given the growing immigration court backlog, ICE could be progressively less inclined to pursue complex criminal-related grounds for deportation instead of immigration-only related grounds. It could be that ICE has already deported many immigrants with criminal histories resulting in fewer immigrants in court who have criminal records, or it could be that immigrants are simply committing fewer crimes. It is certainly not because DHS is filing fewer deportation cases in court. In FY 2013, the immigration courts received 200,000 new deportation cases. By FY 2019, that number more than doubled to about 500,000.

As the first of TRAC's reports on criminal-related charges in immigration court, these new data expand transparency surrounding the role of criminal histories in deportation cases and raise important questions for further research.

Table 1. Number of Criminal-Related Grounds for Deportation Listed on Notices to Appear by Fiscal Year

FY NTA Received by Immigration Court	Nonadmitted Immigrants in Removal Proceedings - All Charges From INA § 212(a)(2)	Admitted Immigrants in Removal Proceedings - All Charges From INA § 237(a)(2)	Total
2001	17,682	26,570	44,252
2002	17,234	22,640	39,874
2003	19,565	24,561	44,126
2004	20,228	24,565	44,793
2005	23,552	25,001	48,553
2006	21,654	23,664	45,318
2007	23,436	25,872	49,308
2008	24,342	27,282	51,624
2009	27,286	29,771	57,057
2010	27,316	29,883	57,199
2011	23,362	29,017	52,379
2012	19,697	27,500	47,197
2013	15,964	23,819	39,783
2014	12,709	18,566	31,275
2015	11,407	16,492	27,899
2016	9,701	14,144	23,845
2017	8,349	12,799	21,148
2018	7,418	12,834	20,252
2019	6,015	10,360	16,375
2020	3,754	7,875	11,629
2021	2,799	5,895	8,694
2022	1,318	2,163	3,481

Footnotes

[1] See specifically Stumpf, J. (2006). The Crimmigration Crisis: Immigrants, Crime, and Sovereign Power. *American University Law Review*, 367-419, and Hernández, C. (2015). *Crimmigration Law*. Washington, D.C.: ABA Book Publishing.

[2] Immigrants may also be deported through a process known as expedited removal, which is typically reserved for immigrants who arrived recently, who have already been deported, or have committed particularly serious crimes. Expedited removal does not take place through the immigration courts and therefore does not figure into these data.

[3] For more information, see "Aggravated Felonies: An Overview" (https://www.americanimmigrationcouncil.org/research/aggravated-felonies-overview) from the American Immigration Council or the "aggravated felony" entry in Cornell Law School's Legal Information Institute (https://www.law.cornell.edu/definitions/uscode.php?width=840&height=800&iframe=true&def_id=8-USC-2031923285-1201680127&term_occur=999&term_src=).

[4] Padilla v. Kentucky, 599 U.S. 356, 377-378 (2010) (Alito, J. concurring).

[5] https://uscode.house.gov/view.xhtml?req=granuleid:USC-prelim-title8-section1227&num=0&edition=prelim

[6] https://uscode.house.gov/view.xhtml?req=granuleid:USC-prelim-title8-section1182&num=0&edition=prelim]

Immigrants Are Less Likely to Commit Crimes

Some Americans believe that undocumented immigrants are a criminal threat to society. Former President Donald J. Trump has leveraged this assumption to inflame the rhetoric around immigration from the U.S.-Mexico border.

A study co-led by Northwestern University economist Elisa Jácome provides the first historical comparison of incarceration rates of immigrants to U.S.-born citizens.

Using incarceration rates as a proxy for crime, a team of economists analyzed 150 years of U.S. Census data and found immigrants were consistently less likely to be incarcerated than people born in the U.S.

They also found beginning in 1960, the incarceration gap widened such that immigrants today are 60% less likely to be incarcerated than the U.S.-born.

continued on next page

"Our study shows that since 1870, it has never been the case that immigrants as a group have been more incarcerated than the U.S.-born," Jácome said. (Jácome is an assistant professor of economics and a faculty fellow with the Institute for Policy Research at Northwestern.)

A multi-university team of economists had previously studied the upward mobility of immigrants and found that children of low-income immigrants tended to be more upwardly mobile than U.S.-born children of low-income families.

Prompted by frequent questions about the impact of immigration on local crime rates, the researchers used data from the U.S. Census to find out whether immigrants were more likely to commit crimes than the U.S.-born.

Starting with the 1870 U.S. Census — the first to include the full population including those formerly enslaved — through the most recent in 2020, which collects data nationwide including from correctional facilities, the researchers measured the gaps between immigrant and U.S.-born levels of incarceration.

Over that 150-year period they found that immigrants' incarceration rate was only slightly lower than that of U.S.-born men. However, in the more recent time period, immigrants are 60% less likely to be incarcerated than U.S. born citizens, and 30% less likely relative to U.S. born whites.

To explain what happened beginning in 1960, Jácome and co-authors point to globalization and skill-based technological changes as coinciding with the gap.

"A surprising finding was the extent to which immigrants with lower levels of education today are significantly less likely to commit crimes than their U.S.-born counterparts," Jácome said. "This may indicate immigrants are more resistant to economic shocks that have affected less-educated men in recent decades."

The researchers say policymakers should consider a variety of factors in addressing immigration issues.

"The impact of immigration on the economy is a multifaceted topic and crime is just one of the factors," Jácome said. "To get a holistic picture, policymakers should also account for research, invention and services that are being provided because of immigrants.

"To the extent you want to make a cost-benefit statement about immigration, you must also look at benefits lost if immigration was reduced."

The study co-authors are Ran Abramitzky, professor of economics at Stanford University; Leah Boustan, professor of economics at Princeton University; Santiago Pérez, associate professor of economics at the University of California at Davis; and Juan David Torres, doctoral student in economics at Stanford.

"Law-Abiding Immigrants: The Incarceration Gap Between Immigrants and the U.S.-born, 1850–2020" was released as a working paper by the National Bureau of Economic Research in July 2023, and will be published in the American Economic Review.

"Immigrants are significantly less likely to commit crimes than the U.S. Born" by Stephanie Kulke, Northwestern University, March 12, 2024.

Viewpoint 4

> *"Putting undocumented immigrants on a pathway to citizenship would increase U.S. GDP by up to $1.7 trillion over the next decade, raise wages for all Americans, and create hundreds of thousands of new jobs, advancing the country's economic recovery."*

Citizenship for Undocumented Immigrants Would Boost U.S. Economic Growth

Giovanni Peri and Reem Zaiour

In this viewpoint, Giovanni Peri and Reem Zaiour present the claim that granting citizenship to undocumented immigrants would allow the U.S. economy to grow overall. They have based their claims on an aggregate macro-growth simulation that modeled several different scenarios – giving citizenship to a) all undocumented immigrants, b) those working in essential roles only, c) those eligible for the American Dream and Promise Act only, and d) those from either group b or c.

As you read, consider the following questions:

1. Which modeled scenario appears to provide the most benefit to both undocumented immigrants and the country as a whole? Why do you think this is so?
2. Is there any implicit source of bias in the authors' motivations behind performing this study? If so, how does this change your analysis of their conclusions?
3. What larger benefits, beyond the direct economic ones discussed in the article, do the authors mention?

Today, 10.2 million undocumented immigrants are living and working in communities across the United States. On average, they have lived in this country for 16 years and are parents, grandparents, and siblings to another 10.2 million family members. At the same time, it has been nearly 40 years since Congress has meaningfully reformed the U.S. immigration system, leaving a generation of individuals and their families vulnerable. Poll after poll has illustrated that the vast majority of Americans support putting undocumented immigrants on a pathway to citizenship. And as the nation emerges from the COVID-19 pandemic and looks toward the future, legalization is a key component of a just, equitable, and robust recovery.

As the Biden administration and Congress craft their recovery legislation and consider how best to move the nation's policies toward a more fair, humane, and workable immigration system, the Center for American Progress and the University of California, Davis's Global Migration Center modeled the economic impacts of several proposals that are currently before Congress. Using an aggregate macro-growth simulation, the model illustrates the benefits to the whole nation from putting undocumented immigrants on a pathway to citizenship. Such legislation would increase productivity and wages—not just for those eligible for legalization, but for all American workers—create hundreds of thousands of jobs, and increase tax revenue.

To help inform policymakers and advocates, this report looks at four potential scenarios where Congress grants a pathway to citizenship to: all undocumented immigrants; undocumented immigrants working in essential occupations; Dreamers and those eligible for Temporary Protected Status (TPS); and a combination of Dreamers, those eligible for TPS, and essential workers.

The report finds that during the next decade:

Scenario 1: Providing a pathway to citizenship for all undocumented immigrants in the United States would boost U.S. gross domestic product (GDP) by a cumulative total of $1.7 trillion over 10 years and create 438,800 new jobs.

- Five years after implementation, those eligible would earn annual wages that are $4,300 higher.
- Ten years after implementation, those annual wages would be $14,000 higher, and all other American workers would see their annual wages increase by $700.

Scenario 2: Providing a pathway to citizenship for undocumented immigrants who are essential workers would boost the GDP by a cumulative total of $989 billion over 10 years and create 203,200 new jobs.

- Five years after implementation, those eligible would experience annual wages that are $4,300 higher.
- Ten years after implementation, those annual wages would be $11,800 higher, and all other American workers would see their annual wages increase by $300.

Scenario 3: Enacting the American Dream and Promise Act (H.R. 6) would increase U.S. GDP by a cumulative total of $799 billion over 10 years and create 285,400 new jobs.

- Five years after implementation, those eligible would experience annual wages that are $4,300 higher.
- Ten years after implementation, those annual wages would be $16,800 higher, and all other American workers would see their annual wages increase by $400.

Scenario 4: Providing a pathway to citizenship for H.R. 6-eligible and undocumented essential workers would boost the GDP by a cumulative total of $1.5 trillion over 10 years and create 400,800 new jobs.

- Five years after implementation, those eligible would experience annual wages that are $4,300 higher.
- Ten years after implementation, those annual wages would be $13,500 higher, and all other American workers would see their annual wages increase by $600.

Importantly, this analysis considers only these direct economic benefits. The model does not capture the potentially large additional benefits to eligible immigrants' children in education, health, and future productivity gains, as these effects would take place likely more than 10 years from implementation.

As the findings above show, creating a pathway to citizenship for undocumented immigrants not only is the right thing to do but also would be a substantial stimulus to the U.S. economy. Undocumented immigrants are critical to the nation's social infrastructure—a fact that has become even more widely understood amid the coronavirus pandemic. Across the country, they are building families and starting businesses, they are keeping hospitals open and functioning, and they are caring for Americans' loved ones. To that extent, legalization and a pathway to citizenship—which would raise wages for all workers, create hundreds of thousands of new jobs, and boost the GDP—is an investment in the country's infrastructure in and of itself. As the United States continues to address the coronavirus pandemic and works toward a just and equitable recovery, Congress must consider these proposals.

Undocumented immigrants are embedded in the United States' infrastructure

Undocumented immigrants have long been essential to the nation's economic growth and prosperity. As the country battled the coronavirus pandemic and economic fallout over the past year, the role of undocumented immigrants in ensuring the well-being and safety of all Americans formed part of the national conversation surrounding essential work. Nearly 3 in 4 undocumented individuals in the workforce—an estimated 5 million—are essential workers. At great risk to themselves and their families, these individuals keep food supply chains running; care for patients in hospitals and support medical systems; maintain the country's roads and buildings; provide critical care and services for children and the elderly; and educate future generations of Americans. All are critical members of the human infrastructure that powers the nation each day.

Despite playing a pivotal role in keeping the country functioning, undocumented immigrants are among the communities hardest hit by COVID-19 and have been continually excluded from past economic recovery efforts and aid programs, all while living under the daily threat of deportation. The reality is that the United States will not rebuild an economy that works for all until it recognizes the ways undocumented immigrants have contributed to the country's success, and economic recovery legislation considers the needs of the undocumented community. As this report details, legalization and a pathway to citizenship would provide the necessary relief and security for undocumented families and would bring a much-needed boost to the U.S. economy.

Parameters used to model impacts of legalization and citizenship for the undocumented

In order to model the economic effects of legalization and a pathway to citizenship for undocumented immigrants, one must first identify who would be eligible. Using the 2019 and 2020 Current Population Survey's (CPS) Annual Social and Economic Supplement (ASEC) conducted by the U.S. Census Bureau, the authors identified 10.2 million undocumented immigrants living in the United States. Using an average of these two years of data allowed the authors to establish a picture of the undocumented workforce both before and at the onset of the pandemic, providing a more realistic picture of the undocumented labor force as the country recovers.

Once the authors established the eligible population, they considered the previous literature on the economic impacts of legalization and citizenship for undocumented immigrants on a host of different inputs. The authors based calculations on a model of economic growth with documented and undocumented workers; human capital depending on labor effectiveness and schooling; and total factor productivity, which depends positively on average human capital. They include:

- A 10 percent wage bump from legalization
- An additional 5 percent wage bump that comes from citizenship
- Productivity increases resulting from additional educational attainment and on-the-job training

What this model measures

Using the conditions described above, the model simulates the effects that legalization and naturalization would have on four segments of the undocumented adult population. Such policies result in permanent changes in labor effectiveness, productivity, and capital investments that are evaluated in a model of an economy growing in a balanced trajectory. The model includes estimates of the effect on average wages of eligible workers, average wages of all other workers, GDP, and number of permanent new jobs using—as base measure of employment—an average of the 2019 and 2020 CPS ASEC.

These effects are estimated for two time frames: the short- to medium-term run (the first five years after implementation) and the long-term run (five to 10 years after implementation).

Short- to medium-run effects

Short-run effects derive mainly from increased productivity of legalized workers. These individuals can move to higher-paying jobs, improve the effectiveness and productivity of their skills, and are less constrained in job searches and opportunities. At the same time, their increased income and spending leads to businesses in their communities being more willing to invest and to take advantage of increased purchasing power that raises returns to investments. This generates increased consumption and demand and higher returns to investment, and it leads to additional investment and production capacity.

Long-run effects

Additional effects need to be considered in the longer run of these policy implementations. On this time horizon, younger undocumented immigrants see their additional schooling translate to higher wages and productivity, especially as one of the ways through which Dreamers can pursue citizenship is by attaining additional education or degrees. These educational advances generate higher efficiency and adoption of better technology and innovation. Other legalized workers are likely to improve their on-the-jobs skills, including their language abilities. In addition to these gains, naturalization, which is likely to occur in this five- to 10-year window, leads to further gains, access to more jobs, and additional wage gains.

This increased human capital in turn increases productivity at established businesses and in local economies. It will also stimulate investments in new businesses and increase productivity and wages of other workers as well as generate permanent new jobs.

Findings from the 4 scenarios

Scenario 1: All undocumented immigrants

Who is eligible in this scenario?

Under this scenario, all undocumented immigrants would be eligible for immediate legalization and a five-year path toward naturalization. The model includes all undocumented workers along with Dreamers, regardless of work status. The authors estimate that 7.7 million of the 10.2 million undocumented individuals eligible for protection using 2019–2020 CPS data were either employed in the year prior to the COVID-19 crisis or were Dreamers.

Short-run impacts (implementation to year five):

- Increase in annual wages of undocumented workers: $4,300 (10 percent)

Long-run impacts (year five to year 10):

- Increase in annual wages of undocumented workers: $14,000 (32.4 percent)
- Increase in annual wages of all other workers: $700 (1.1 percent)

Total cumulative GDP increase through the decade: $1.7 trillion
Total number of new jobs created: 438,800

Scenario 2: Undocumented immigrants working in essential roles

Who is eligible in this scenario?

Under this scenario, all undocumented immigrants working in essential jobs, as defined by the U.S. Department of Homeland Security (DHS), would be eligible to legalize immediately and access a pathway to citizenship after five years. The authors estimate that 5 million undocumented individuals are eligible for protection using 2019–2020 CPS data.

Short-run impacts (implementation to year five):

- Increase in annual wages of undocumented workers: $4,300 (10 percent)

Long-run impacts (year five to year 10):

- Increase in annual wages of undocumented workers: $11,800 (27.3 percent)
- Increase in annual wages of all other workers: $300 (0.5 percent)

Total cumulative GDP increase through the decade: $989 billion
Total number of new jobs created: 203,200

Scenario 3: Undocumented immigrants eligible for the American Dream and Promise Act

Who is eligible under this scenario?

Undocumented immigrants are considered eligible for a conditional permanent resident status under the Dream provisions of the law if they arrived in the United States prior to 2021 at the age of 18 or younger and have a high school diploma or are enrolled in high school. They are eligible for permanent residency after completing any of the following three criteria: two years of study toward an advanced degree or technical training; two years of military service; or three years of employment, 75 percent of which must be performed while work authorized. The authors estimate that 2 million undocumented individuals are eligible for protection using 2019–2020 CPS data.

Undocumented immigrants are considered eligible under the Promise provisions of the law if they were eligible for either TPS as of September 2017 or Deferred Enforced Departure as of January 2021.

Short-run impacts (implementation to year five):

- Increase in annual wages of undocumented workers: $4,300 (10 percent)

Long-run impacts (year five to year 10):

- Increase in annual wages of undocumented workers: $16,800 (38.9 percent)
- Increase in annual wages of all other workers: $400 (0.7 percent)

Total cumulative GDP growth through the decade: $799 billion
Total number of new jobs created: 285,400

Scenario 4: Undocumented immigrants who are either essential workers or eligible for the American Dream and Promise Act

Who is eligible under this scenario?

Undocumented immigrants who were either employed as essential workers or eligible for the American Dream and Promise Act are eligible for legalization and a pathway to citizenship. Undocumented immigrants are considered eligible for a conditional permanent resident status under the Dream provisions of the law if they arrived in the United States prior to 2021 at the age of 18 or younger and have a high school diploma or are enrolled in high school. They are eligible for permanent residency after completing any of the following three criteria: two years of study toward an advanced degree or technical training; two years of military service; or three years of employment, 75 percent of which must be performed while work authorized. Undocumented immigrants are considered eligible under the Promise provisions of the law if they were eligible for either TPS as of September 2017 or Deferred Enforced Departure as of January 2021. The authors estimate that 6 million undocumented individuals are eligible for protection using 2019–2020 CPS data.

Short-run impacts (implementation to year five):

- Increase in annual wages of undocumented workers: $4,300 (10 percent)

Long-run impacts (year five to year 10):

- Increase in annual wages of undocumented workers: $13,500 (31.3 percent)
- Increase in annual wages of all other workers: $600 (1 percent)

Total cumulative GDP growth through the decade: $1.5 trillion
Total number of new jobs created: 400,800

Conclusion

Undocumented immigrants are longtime members of their communities, and the nation as a whole, and have made significant economic contributions. By putting them on a pathway to citizenship, Congress and the administration can turn those contributions into massive gains for the entire economy and for all workers—by as much as a cumulative $1.7 trillion during the next decade. As Congress debates further recovery and immigration reform legislation, it must include legalization in those discussions.

Periodical and Internet Sources Bibliography

The following articles have been selected to supplement the diverse views presented in this chapter.

Ran Abramitzky, Leah Platt Boustan, Elisa Jacome, Santiago Perez, and Juan David Torres, "Lab-Abiding Immigrants: The Incarceration Gap Between Immigrants and the US-born, 1870-2020," National Bureau of Economic Research, March 2024. https://www.nber.org/papers/w31440.

Jeanne Batalova, "Immigrant Health-Care Workers in the United States," Migration Policy Institute, April 7, 2023. https://www.migrationpolicy.org/article/immigrant-health-care-workers-united-states.

Daniel Bergstresser, "Rising Costs of Financing U.S. Government Debt," Econofact, December 5, 2022. https://econofact.org/rising-costs-of-financing-u-s-government-debt.

Drew DeSilver, "Key facts about the U.S. national debt," Pew Research Center, August 12, 2025. https://www.pewresearch.org/short-reads/2025/08/12/key-facts-about-the-us-national-debt/.

Karen Dynane, "High and Rising US Federal Debt: Causes and Implications," Aspen Institute, November 8, 2023. https://www.economicstrategygroup.org/wp-content/uploads/2023/11/Dynan_2023_Chapter.pdf.

Amy Hsin, " 'Dreamers' could give US economy – and even American workers – a boost", The Conversation, January 19, 2018. https://www.newamericaneconomy.org/wp-content/uploads/2017/07/NAE_UnusualWorkingHours_V5.pdf.

"The Long-Term Budget Outlook Under Alternative Scenarios for the Economy and the Budget", Congressional Budget Office, July 20, 2023. https://www.cbo.gov/publication/59233.

Jack Malde, Theresa Cardinal Brown, and Ben Gitis, "Green Light to Growth: Estimating the Economic Benefits of Green Card Backlogs," Bipartisan Policy Center, Washington, D.C., November 8, 2023. https://bipartisanpolicy.org/report/green-light-to-growth-estimating-the-economic-benefits-of-clearing-green-card-backlogs/.

Lawrence Mishel and Josh Bivens, "Identifying the policy levers generating wage suppression and wage inequality," Economic Policy Institute, May, 13 2021. https://www.epi.org/unequalpower/publications/wage-suppression-inequality/.

"On The Clock: How Immigrants Fill Gaps in the Labor Market by Working Nontraditional Hours," New American Economy, July 2017. https://www.newamericaneconomy.org/wp-content/uploads/2017/07/NAE_UnusualWorkingHours_V5.pdf.

Chapter 3

Who Should Be Allowed to Immigrate?

Chapter Preface

People make the decision to leave their homeland for many different reasons. Some are fleeing persecution, oppression, or violence; some desire better economic opportunities; some are simply in search of a change in culture or experience.

But should their reasons for emigrating from their homelands be considered when deciding whether to allow them to enter the United States? This is the main question addressed by the viewpoints in this chapter.

Some viewpoints discuss Americans' historical tradition of welcoming all comers, reflecting their country's reputation as a "melting pot" where anyone with the motivation and dedication can pursue and achieve the widely-touted American Dream. In some cases, they argue that the United States is both morally and legally obligated to accept refugees.

Other viewpoints remind us of the necessity for compassion towards immigrants, who are not only starting their lives over from scratch, but in many cases arriving from countries torn apart by war and privation.

Still others point out potential pitfalls of completely open borders, such as an influx of criminals or other potential undesirable elements. In addition, this chapter presents a closer look at how some immigrants who are seen as "undesirable" have been treated in recent years. Readers who are attentive to the issues raised in this chapter may find themselves questioning their own previously-held beliefs in the face of some immigrants' experiences.

VIEWPOINT 1

"Not only does the US have an international legal obligation to do so…it has an obligation to do so under its own domestic law."

What Legal Obligation Does the United States Have to Accept Refugees?

Liam Thornton

In this viewpoint, Liam Thorton, a lecturer in law at University College Dublin, addresses an executive order signed by President Donald Trump on January 28, 2017, banning a majority of refugees from coming to the United States. This viewpoint, while written in response to a past event, still contains important discussions of the moral and legal obligations all countries have to protect refugees.

As you read, consider the following questions:

1. Is it reasonable to expect the United States to abide by laws passed internationally?
2. What "loopholes", which would technically support the legality of the executive order, does Thorton present?
3. What current immigration policies have stirred up similar debates among the international community?

"Q&A: what legal obligation does the US have to accept refugees?' by The Conversation, January 27, 2017.

Donald Trump signed an executive order on January 27 [2017], which temporarily bans the majority of refugees from coming to the US and suspends visas for those from seven, mainly Muslim, countries. The Conversation asked Liam Thornton, lecturer in law at University College Dublin, whether the plans breach international law.

If a person arrives on US soil and claims asylum, does the US have to deal with their claim under international law?

Yes. Not only does the US have an international legal obligation to do so, based on the requirement of complying with the object and purpose of the 1951 Refugee Convention, and implementing legal obligations in good faith, it has an obligation to do so under its own domestic law.

The executive order cannot displace domestic legal obligations. So those who, with great difficulty, manage to reach the US will have to have their asylum claims examined. The duty not to return a person to a state where they may face torture or other serious harms is absolute under the UN's Convention Against Torture. The US has signed and ratified this convention.

However, with the likely increase in asylum detention of people crossing the US-Mexico border that will arise from one of Trump's earlier executive orders, there is potential for decisions on whether a person is a refugee being made in an exceptionally tight time frame. It's possible that, more generally, asylum decisions will be rushed through and the law not properly adhered to.

Under international law, can the US ban asylum seekers from certain countries? Do experts have something to add to public debate?

We think so.

Under international law, the US cannot ban asylum seekers from certain countries. The US has signed and ratified a number of international treaties that prohibit religious and race discrimination in the operation of legal systems, and this extends to operating a migration system in line with international non-discrimination protections.

That said, a person cannot claim asylum unless they are on US soil. The executive order will generally suspend issuing visas for 90 days for Iranian, Iraqi, Libyan, Somalian, Sudanese, Syrian and Yemeni citizens under the US visa-waiver programme. An exception for "religious minority" – such as Christians from these countries – appears to be nothing more than a poorly attempted disguise to try to ban Muslims from these countries from reaching US soil.

However, this prevention of safe, legal and accessible routes is not unique to the US. In the European Union, the imposition of visa rules for countries that produce the greatest number of refugees, is precisely what is leading thousands of migrants and refugees to make the perilous Mediterranean crossing. So while you have a right to leave your country, all too often your right to claim asylum in another country can be ignored by states through imposing harsh visa requirements which prevent potential refugees arriving in a country and lodging an asylum claim. For example, a Syrian refugee living in Turkey who is unlikely to get a visa to enter Europe's Schengen zone, may choose to resort to crossing the Mediterranean in a boat.

Why is the refugee admissions programme being paused?

The US Refugee Admissions Programme (USRAP) deals with people referred from the UNHCR, a US embassy or assigned non-governmental organisations, or a limited direct application scheme. It is open to people who already have refugee status (or would be likely to qualify), who are outside the US, but may wish the US to consider them for entry as a resettled refugee. The US had been due to take in 110,000 refugees under USRAP in 2017, but in the executive order Trump indicates he wants this number to be more than halved to an intake of 50,000 refugees. The executive order calls for USRAP to be paused for all refugee applicants for a period of

120 days. The reason Trump offers for this suspension is to ensure the already complex vetting processes are strengthened.

The US takes the largest number of people under UNHCR's resettlement programme. Looking to international law, there is no legal obligation to have or operate a resettlement programme.

Yet, an exceptionally concerning aspect of the executive order is to exclude Syrian refugees from being resettled in the US under USRAP. This exclusion is to remain in place until such time as Trump has determined that entry of Syrian refugees aligns "with the national interest". Trump has proposed that "safe zones" are to be planned for refugees within Syria as a result of the Syrian citizen exclusion from USRAP.

How many asylum seekers are we talking about?

From 2013 to 2015, only 1,823 Syrian refugees were accepted under USRAP. Therefore, Syrian refugees constituted an exceptionally small number of the almost 210,000 refugees accepted for resettlement in the US between 2013 and 2015. Outside of USRAP, the number of individual Syrians claiming asylum on the territory of the US between 2013 and 2015 was exceptionally low. This is because visa laws already in place manage to deflect most Syrian asylum applicants from ever reaching the US. The proposed visa prohibition will mean the numbers of Syrians claiming asylum at US borders will decrease.

What means does the international community have to punish the US if it breaches international refugee or asylum law?

Well, that is the significant issue with international legal obligations and domestic enforcement of these obligations. International refugee and international human rights law relies heavily on attempting to embarrass or pressure a state to comply with their international legal obligations. This can have some effect on smaller states – for example in Ireland, the UN Human Rights Committee added to the chorus of activist agitation for seeking to change misogynistic laws on abortion.

However, a country as powerful as the US can easily set aside international legal obligations to which they had previously adhered. So I would be surprised to see any "punishment" from the international community. If the international community is genuinely outraged by this decision, other countries need to start planning to increase their own refugee resettlement programmes, along with ensuring safe, legal and accessible routes of entry for those seeking sanctuary. But, given the current political climate in Europe, Australia and elsewhere, I'd expect a rather muted response to the executive order.

This article was updated on January 28th after the executive order, a draft of which had been widely leaked, was signed.

Trump Promised the "Largest Deportation" in U.S. History. Here's How He Might Start.

Morning Edition is diving into promises President-elect Donald Trump said he would fulfill in his second term. NPR's Steve Inskeep asks immigration policy expert Andrew Selee about Trump's pledge to deport millions of immigrants.

What Trump said about deporting immigrants

While campaigning, President-elect Donald Trump promised "On day one, I will launch the largest deportation program of criminals in the history of America." He referenced 1954's "Operation Wetback," an effort ordered by President Dwight D. Eisenhower. Government estimates showed more than a million Mexican immigrants and some U.S. citizens were rounded up. The program got its official name from a racist term for Mexicans who swam or waded across the Rio Grande.

He also said he would use the Alien Enemies Act of 1798 to precipitate the removal of undocumented migrants from the U.S. and "dismantle every migrant criminal network operating on American soil" at an Oct. 25 campaign rally.

continued on next page

Trump may start by trying to remove newer arrivals and expanding deportation guidelines

Andrew Selee, president of the Migration Policy Institute, said Trump's mass deportation plan could begin with the removal of hundreds of thousands of new arrivals admitted under programs instituted by President Biden.

"The first thing we know he will almost certainly do is cancel humanitarian parole for people that received it, people who came through CBP One, this app that people use to schedule an appointment to come across the border," Selee said.

He also pointed to the possibility of Trump going after people with Temporary Protected Status, a limited status offered to people displaced from their home countries by extreme circumstances, and people admitted under a program offered to Cubans, Venezuelans, Haitians and Nicaraguans.

Selee also said Trump could change deportation guidelines for Immigrations and Customs Enforcement so that the agency can arrest and put undocumented immigrants in deportation proceedings more freely.

"That is something that changed under the Biden administration, where they were primarily pursuing people who had criminal records or people who are a threat to national security," Selee said.

Selee also says Trump has talked about expanding detention facilities, "But whether he'll be able to use military bases or not or other federal facilities and whether he will try and use the military itself, and that would require going back to the [Alien Enemies Act of 1798]."

Trump could argue for using of the more than 200-year-old law to override due process and justify using military support for arresting and holding people without legal status.

Selee added that people living in Republican-controlled states are much more likely to see enforcement actions.

"We saw that during the last Trump administration. There were very successful enforcement efforts against people who are here illegally in red states because local law enforcement was willing to collaborate," Selee said.

He added that, though law enforcement in blue states didn't outright refuse to cooperate, they didn't put large amounts of resources into collaborating with immigration enforcement.

What Trump's team says

NPR asked the Trump transition team if the president-elect had more specific details on how his plan to carry out mass deportations would begin. Trump transition spokesperson Karoline Leavitt offered the following statement in response:

"The American people re-elected President Trump by a resounding margin giving him a mandate to implement the promises he made on the campaign trail. He will deliver."

Trump's appointments signal seriousness about his enforcement actions

This week, Trump announced he would make Tom Homan his "border czar" overseeing the north and south U.S. borders. Homan led ICE in an acting capacity for about a year and a half during his first term. Border czar is not an official cabinet position and it's unclear exactly what role Homan would take.

Before the election, Homan said enforcement would focus on immigrants who pose "public safety threats and the national security threats first." He also indicated more workplace raids could happen.

A CBS journalist asked Homan during an October interview if family separations could be avoided during mass deportations, particularly in the case of U.S. citizen children with undocumented parents. Homan responded by saying "Families can be deported together."

Trump also announced the expected return of Stephen Miller, the hardline immigration restrictionist who is seen as the architect of the Muslim travel ban and the controversial "zero tolerance" policy that separated thousands of children from their parents at the southern border. The reunification of some 1,400 children with their families had not been confirmed as of April this year.

South Dakota Gov. Kristi Noem was also tapped to lead Homeland Security, the cabinet that oversees immigration benefits and enforcement. Noem deployed National Guard troops to the U.S.-Mexico border several times in recent years.

"Trump promised the 'largest deportation' in U.S. history. Here's how he might start" by Steve Inskeep and Christopher Thomas, National Public Radio Inc. (NPR), November 14, 2024.

VIEWPOINT 2

> *"A firm wouldn't hire only on the basis of age, years of work and years of education. Our immigration system shouldn't work that way either."*

Should the United States Adopt a Merit-Based Immigration System?

Julia Gelatt and Jeremy L. Neufield

In the following viewpoint, Julia Gelatt and Jeremy L. Neufield debate whether or not the United States should start using a merit-based immigration system that would only admit people deemed "valuable contributors" by virtue of their education, ability to work, or age, among other potential factors. They each argue one side of the issue, with Gelatt arguing "for" and Neufield arguing "against."

As you read, consider the following questions:

1. Which side do you feel has the stronger arguments?
2. Do you think language skills should be a determining factor in who is allowed into the United States?
3. Why is it important to keep the definition of "merit" broad?

"Should the U.S. Adopt a Merit-Based Immigration System" by Julia Gelatt and Jeremy L. Neufeld, SHRM, May 28, 2020. Reprinted by Permission.

YES: Merit-based immigration is good for the country and for U.S. employers—when merit is defined broadly.

Since his days on the campaign trail, President Donald Trump has pressed for what he refers to as "merit-based" immigration. He has praised Canada's points-based selection system and endorsed proposed legislation that would prioritize immigrants with the strongest English skills, highest education levels and highest-paying job offers. He's right: The U.S. should select more of its immigrants on the basis of merit. But the definition of "merit" should include the value of needed workers across the entire skills spectrum.

Essential Workers

Before COVID-19 and the resulting economic calamity and border closings, U.S. employers were hiring about 450,000 new immigrant workers per year. These workers fill a wide range of jobs, from farmwork, food processing and construction to research science and medicine. The response to the coronavirus has brought into stark relief how essential many of these occupations are.

Whatever the coming economic recovery looks like, employers will rely on immigration for needed workers. Indeed, given the aging of the U.S. population and declining birthrate, immigrants and their U.S.-born children are projected to drive all growth in the working-age population through 2035.

Most foreign workers arrive outside of official employment-based channels. The current employer-sponsored immigration system brings in only 140,000 long-term, employment-based immigrants each year, and about half of those are the spouses and children of selected workers. The current system is also strongly skewed toward higher-skilled immigrants: Most employment-based green cards require a college education or advanced degree; only 5,000 are available for employers that want to sponsor low-skilled workers.

The U.S. also allows employers to bring in hundreds of thousands of temporary employees, including farmworkers, high-skilled H-1B workers and other seasonal workers (to fill summer resort and landscaping jobs, for example). But firms that want to keep these workers on long-term have very limited channels to do so. The system is not well-aligned with the interests of U.S. businesses, immigrant workers or the economy overall.

Redefining Merit

The U.S. needs a reformed merit-based immigration system that is more flexible—with "merit" defined as the ability to contribute positively to the nation's economy. And merit-based immigration need not involve a points-based system. In times when there is a demonstrated need for workers by a particular employer or in a particular job sector, immigrant workers with needed skills should be admitted in greater numbers—whether those skills are rapidly picking and bundling radishes, caring for the elderly, or conducting scientific research or engineering studies. Annual limits should be flexible, expanding when labor markets are tight and contracting when jobs are scarce.

A merit-based system should also preserve a primary role for employers in choosing desired workers. In Canada, Australia and other countries with traditional points-based systems, initial selection of workers based on factors such as language skills, educational attainment and field of work led to high levels of "brain waste"—the problem of foreign-trained doctors driving taxis, for example. Over time, these systems were changed to prioritize workers with in-country experience and employment offers. The U.S. system has much lower levels of brain waste. That's because employers are the best judges of which workers are poised to succeed in their line of work.

A broader, more flexible merit-based immigration stream would supply employers with needed workers, support U.S. workforce growth amid an aging population and bolster overall U.S. economic growth. To build a successful merit-based system, we must recognize that there is merit in many different types of skills and that employers, rather than governments, are best at evaluating who has merit.

NO: Points-based immigration offers limited risks, but there are better options for dynamism and growth.

Merit-based immigration built on a points system offers low risk but only limited returns. It increases the value generated by the median immigrant but is not designed to capitalize on immigrant entrepreneurship, fails to recognize nontraditional sources of talent and inadequately integrates many immigrants into the economy. To promote long-term economic growth, the U.S. can afford to take more risks in pursuit of higher rewards.

Superstars and Startups

The typical way to think about the benefits of immigration is to assume that the value of immigrants rises in proportion to their education, experience and other traditional qualifications. It's easy to see why points-based systems are attractive: Raise the average skill level among immigrants, and you raise the value of your immigration system proportionally.

But this ignores the potential of—and the immense opportunities that flow from—immigrant superstars. One entrepreneur with a billion- dollar idea may generate more value than thousands of dependable, hardworking, high-skilled workers.

Traditional merit-based systems are not designed with superstars in mind. Points-based systems value tried-and-true characteristics and reward applicants who follow reliable, well-traveled paths. These systems raise the value created by the median immigrant, but they may thin the ranks of outliers who generate considerably more value. Superstar entrepreneurs are more likely to make precisely the types of risky career decisions that hurt their chances under a points-based selection system.

Points-based and other immigration systems that focus on raising the median skill level of immigrants are great for improving efficiency at the margin; they're just not designed to bring in new, industry-disrupting ideas.

Decentralizing the Talent Search

If we're willing to give up the idea of a points-based system and the security and safety it offers, our immigration system can take advantage of a decentralized search for talent undertaken by investors and employers.

For example, a startup visa could piggyback on the judgment and discretion of investors who have the means, incentive and skill to identify immigrants with superstar potential. The program could offer visas to immigrant entrepreneurs who want to launch startups in the U.S. and who have raised a certain amount of investment capital.

Notably, Australia, Canada and New Zealand, often held up as models for immigration reform by proponents of points-based immigration, have all found that points-based systems are insufficient for entrepreneurship. As a result, each of those nations runs a startup visa program in parallel with its points-based system.

Employer Sponsorship

Even outside the market for superstars, points-based systems can be static in the face of changing market conditions. That is why it is vital to retain employer sponsorship, with reforms to ensure that scarce visas go to employers with the greatest needs. That approach provides a level of flexibility that a points-based system would be unable to match.

Additionally, ensuring that immigrants to the U.S. have jobs waiting for them helps them better integrate into the economy. For all of the weaknesses of its immigration program, the U.S. historically has had a lower foreign-born unemployment rate than countries with typical merit-based systems. It should be no surprise that countries with points-based systems have introduced reforms that give extra weight to applicants with existing job offers.

Ultimately, what the case for points-based immigration misses is what every HR professional already understands: There's no one simple scorecard to identify talent. A firm wouldn't hire only on the basis of age, years of work and years of education. Our immigration system shouldn't work that way either.

Viewpoint 3

> *"The head of the Tahirih Justice Centre in Houston said she had seen cases where parents had not been told ahead of time that their child was being taken away, and instead were told by immigration officers that their child required a bath, only to not be returned."*

Viewpoints on the Treatment of Immigrants

BBC News

In the following article, BBC News presents information about visits paid by several lawmakers and politicians to migrant detention camps in 2018. This viewpoint addresses the policy at the time of separating migrant children from their parents and holding them in separate facilities, as well as the general conditions at those facilities, and the lawmakers' responses to what they observed during their visits.

As you read, consider the following questions:

1. Based on what was reported in the article, were the responses of the lawmakers consistent across the board, or did lawmakers from different parties have different responses to what they saw?

2. In general, do the conditions at the facilities described in the article seem to meet a reasonable standard of care?
3. Do you think these immigrants would have been treated differently if they came from another part of the world?

Reporters and Democratic lawmakers have been allowed inside a detention centre that lies at the heart of a growing storm over a new US policy separating migrant children from their parents.

Authorities did not allow photos or videos to be taken inside the centre, but US Customs and Border Protection later released several images. Former First Lady Laura Bush has compared it to the internment camps used for Japanese-Americans during World War Two. A Democratic congressman who visited the site said it was "nothing short of a prison".

The Texas facility is known as Ursula, though immigrants are reportedly calling it La Perrera - dog kennel in Spanish - in reference to the cages used to hold children and adults who have ended up there after crossing the border from Mexico illegally.

"One cage had 20 children inside. Scattered about are bottles of water, bags of chips [crisps] and large foil sheets intended to serve as blankets," the Associated Press reports.

Democratic Senator Jeff Merkley led the team of lawmakers to the site in the town of McAllen on Sunday.

He hit the headlines earlier this month when he was turned away from another facility housing some 1,500 boys in a disused Walmart store.

Speaking to CNN after the visit to Ursula, he said: "In wire-mesh, chain linked cages that are about 30x30 [feet], a lot of young folks put into them.

"I must say though, far fewer than I was here two weeks ago. I was told that buses full (of children) were taken away before I arrived.

"That was one of my concerns, that essentially, when you have to give lengthy notice, you end up a little bit of a show rather than seeing what's really going on in these centres."

Maryland Senator Chris Van Hollen and Vermont Congressman Peter Welch expressed shock and anger over the conditions they saw [as posted on X]:

- **Senator Chris Van Hollen** – *Just left Border Patrol Processing Center in McAllen – aka "the dog kennel." Witnessed loads of kids massed together in large pens of chain-linked fence separated from their moms and dads. @realDonaldTrump, change your shameful policy today! #FamiliesBelongTogether*
- **Senator Peter Welch** – *I just exited a border patrol "processing facility" known as the "icebox." It is nothing short of a prison. I saw chain link cages full of unaccompanied children. They sat on metal benches and stared straight ahead silently.*

Inside Ursula, more than 1,100 illegal immigrants are waiting to be processed. They have been separated into three wings: unaccompanied children, lone adults and parents with their children. Officials said nearly 200 of those being held there were unaccompanied minors and another 500 were parents with their children.

The *Los Angeles Times*, which also sent a team there, described the 72,000 sq ft facility as "clean and spare, with bare concrete floors".

A patrol agent currently in charge of the site, John Lopez, told the paper the 42 portable toilets on site are cleaned three times a day. There are three paramedics, two medical members of staff and 310 employees - but no mental health staff, or training, the paper notes. The main lights in the building remain on at all times.

Nearly 60 miles away, in the town of Brownsville, some 1,500 boys are being housed inside a building that was once a Walmart superstore. The boys, aged 10 to 17, were all caught illegally crossing the border. It is America's largest facility for such minors, and numbers have increased in the past month by several hundred.

Senator Merkley's Facebook Live on 4 June showing security officials denying him entry to that site - known as Casa Padre - led to questions about conditions there. Last week, news organisations were given a tour.

No cages were mentioned, but the accommodation was likened to dorm rooms inside a giant warehouse. To accommodate for the growing numbers since the new "zero-tolerance" policy went into force, cots have been added to sleeping areas in the Casa Padre.

The *New York Times* described it as "clean, massive and brightly lit", with the children given classes six hours each week day and outdoor play time for two hours a day. They have 48 medical staff and three on call doctors on hand.

Long-term trauma?

"Those kids inside who have been separated from their parents are already being traumatised," Senator Merkley warned. "It doesn't matter whether the floor is swept and the bed-sheets tucked in tight."

Officials say they are trying to keep siblings together and not separate children under four or younger from their parents.

But Anne Chandler, who's running a non-profit project for migrant children found on the southern US border, told Texas Monthly she had heard stories of "kids that are very young, that are breastfeeding babies and under three in the shelters, separated from their parents".

The head of the Tahirih Justice Centre in Houston said she had seen cases where parents had not been told ahead of time that their child was being taken away, and instead were told by immigration officers that their child required a bath, only to not be returned.

"I was talking to one mother, and she said, "Don't take my child away," and the child started screaming and vomiting and crying hysterically, and she asked the officers, "Can I at least have five minutes to console her?" They said no," Ms Chandler told the magazine.

A rights worker who visited the Ursula facility at the weekend told the Associated Press she had spoken to a 16-year-old girl who was left in charge of an unaccompanied toddler for three days and tasked with changing the child's nappies.

"She had to teach other kids in the cell to change her diaper," Michelle Brane, from the Women's Refugee Commission, said. The girl - who was four years old - was later reunited with her aunt, but the process took time because she did not speak Spanish but a language indigenous to Guatemala, the agency reports.

"She was so traumatised that she wasn't talking," Ms Brane said, describing the girl. "She was just curled up in a little ball."

She is not alone in voicing concerns over the long-term effects of separating adults and their children.

The American Academy of Pediatrics warned last week that "highly stressful experiences, including family separation, can cause irreparable harm to lifelong development by disrupting a child's brain architecture".

Separately, authorities have announced plans to erect tent cities that will hold hundreds more children in the Texas desert where temperatures regularly reach 40C (105F).

Local lawmaker Jose Rodriguez described the plan as "totally inhumane" and "outrageous", adding: "It should be condemned by anyone who has a moral sense of responsibility."

> *"The Fourteenth Amendment gives the right of citizenship to all people born in the U.S. regardless of their parents' nationality."*

Opinions on DACA Recipients and Other Immigrant Groups

Jean Lantz Reisz

In the following viewpoint, Amy Lieberman, a politics editor at The Conversation U.S., asked Jean Lantz Reisz to explain how President Trump could follow through on some of the promises he made during his campaign regarding immigration policies, and potential legal and political obstacles he could encounter along the way.

As you read, consider the following questions:

1. According to Reisz, how much power do the states have to resist federal deportation attempts?
2. What tools does the executive branch have at its disposal to "punish" states who do not assist in deportations?
3. Does the Fourteenth Amendment, as described in the article, offer blanket protection for anyone born on U.S. soil?

What role do states play in any Trump order to deport immigrants?

There are 11 million people living without legal authorization in the U.S., and Trump would have the authority, as president, to deport those people. But it would be very expensive to pay for the immigration officers, immigration judges, detention facilities, the plane flights and more that would be required to do so. Estimates on the cost of mass deportation range from $88 billion a year to more than $300 billion.

The administration is probably going to have to rely on state and local governments to help carry out these deportations. The president cannot legally force state and local governments to cooperate with immigration enforcement. About 10 states, including New York, Massachusetts and California, have laws that prohibit cooperation with Immigration and Customs Enforcement, or ICE – the federal agency that oversees immigration and deportation – under certain circumstances.

For example, in California, employers may not allow ICE to enter nonpublic areas of their workplace without a proper warrant. Other states also prohibit law enforcement from sharing the immigration status of certain low-level criminal offenders.

The federal government could give more money to a state in order to help it cooperate with federal immigration efforts, and take it away if they do not cooperate. But federal case law says that the president does not have the authority to withhold federal money to coerce a state into cooperating with immigration actions.

Could Trump still send federal immigration officers to a state that does not cooperate, in order to identify and detain immigrants?

States could not prevent the federal government from coming in to arrest and deport people – but they don't have to help them, and could set up some obstacles. The federal government would have to provide all of its own personnel. Texas and Arizona have recently approved laws that require local law enforcement to cooperate with the Department of Homeland Security and enforce immigration law.

ICE could rely on local sheriffs or police in some states, like Texas, to identify and arrest immigrants and turn them over to ICE to deport. In other states, like Oregon and Illinois, that want to protect immigrants from deportation, they can refuse to cooperate with federal authorities by not providing certain personal information on immigrants.

What are the other risks immigrants might be concerned about?

There are about 580,000 people who are living in the U.S. and are part of the Deferred Action for Childhood Arrivals, or DACA, program. DACA gives some people who came to the U.S. illegally as children the right to legally work, go to school and live in the country. The courts have already litigated that a president can lawfully terminate DACA through a certain process.

Currently, President Joe Biden is defending DACA by appealing a Texas district court decision that DACA is an unlawful program. Once in office, Trump can instruct the Justice Department to dismiss the appeal, effectively ending DACA.

People who apply for DACA have to state in their application that they are in the country unlawfully. So the government could prove that DACA recipients can legally be deported, and will have information on where they live.

The next group of immigrants that could be targeted is people from Afghanistan and other countries who have humanitarian parole, which is temporary permission to remain in the U.S. legally. Trump can end all of the parole programs, including those for Ukrainians.

In addition, Trump can end Temporary Protected Status, a law that gives temporary permission to some people to legally stay in the U.S. for up to two years because of an emergency situation in their countries. He tried to do this, but was unsuccessful, during his first administration because he didn't follow the right legal process. About 1.2 million people are covered under this program, which Biden expanded.

Trump has said he would end birthright citizenship, which is the right for any person born in the country to get citizenship. Could he legally do this?

The Trump administration could order federal officials to stop processing passports and Social Security numbers for people who cannot establish that their parents are U.S. citizens. An ensuing lawsuit, probably brought by individuals denied their documents, would force courts to weigh in on birthright citizenship.

The Fourteenth Amendment gives the right of citizenship to all people born in the U.S. regardless of their parents' nationality. Challengers to birthright citizenship argue that the Fourteenth Amendment should be reinterpreted to exclude people who were born in the U.S. to parents who are present unlawfully and therefore without the consent of the U.S. government.

To succeed in overturning birthright citizenship, the Supreme Court would have to reverse a 126-year-old precedent, which states that anyone who is born on U.S. soil and not the child of someone engaged in diplomatic service is a U.S. citizen.

Trump has talked about using the Alien Enemies Act as a way to deport people. What does this mean?

Trump has talked about using the Alien Enemies Act of 1798 as a way to get around judicial review and immigration courts and deport people such as gang members and cartel members. This law allows a president, during a time of war, to detain and deport people born in an enemy nation.

One problem with this is that Trump won't have the authority to deport people under this act, unless there is a war with or invasion by another nation or government. Gangs or cartels are not their own nation or government. For example, Trump could not simultaneously recognize the Mexican government and a cartel also as the government of Mexico – or succeed in legally proving the Mexican government is sending cartel members to invade the U.S. on behalf of the Mexican government.

Another problem Trump would have in using the Alien Enemies Act is that it allows for review by the courts to determine whether an individual is actually an "enemy alien." It would not likely provide an automatic shortcut to deportation and would end up in litigation.

VIEWPOINT 5

> *"The reasons people migrate from Northern Central America are complex and interconnected, stretching from economic opportunity to gang violence to ineffective governance."*

A Case Study of Immigrants From Northern Central America

Jenny Villatoro and Matthew Rooney

Here, Jenny Villatoro and Matthew Rooney explain why so many immigrants to the United States come from countries in northern Central America. They suggest that if the U.S. government wishes to address the constant stream of immigrants, it should look to address the root of the problem – the issues within the countries that people are emigrating from – rather than trying to act from a reactionary standpoint by dealing with immigrants once they reach U.S. soil.

As you read, consider the following questions:

1. According to the authors, what are the largest root causes of migration from northern Central America?
2. What obstacles does the United States face if it tries to address the "root" of the immigration problem, rather

"Root Causes of Migration: From Northern Central America" by Jenny Villatoro and Matthew Rooney, George W. Bush Presidential Center, January 17, 2023. Reprinted by Permission.

than just dealing with the immigrants once they have arrived?

3. What recommendations do the authors make for how the United States should deal with the issues presented?

Over 35% of the approximately 1.6 million migrants arriving at our southern border in 2021 were families or unaccompanied children. Almost 200,000 children came from Northern Central America (El Salvador, Guatemala, Honduras), and about half of them were unaccompanied. Shifting demographics, the increase in children and family arrivals, and the increase in large caravans arriving from Northern Central America have spurred a conversation into the root causes of migration.

With billions of dollars of foreign aid and development investment being directed to these countries to address the underlying reasons for migration, it's imperative that stakeholders have an adequate understanding of the depth, complexity, and interconnectedness of these root causes. It's all too easy for the nuances that inform good policy to be superficialized into one-dimensional concepts and lost in the pursuit of quick wins.

The reasons people migrate from Northern Central America are complex and interconnected, stretching from economic opportunity to gang violence to ineffective governance. Some of the most obvious are gender-based violence, poverty, instability, and corruption in their home countries, as well as impunity for violent offenders. There are also more nuanced drivers that help create an environment people either choose to leave or are forced to leave. These include low educational attainment, the influence of remittances, and family reunification. And these are just the "push factors," not the "pull factors" – in particular the presence of a large Central American community in the United States that offers a daily reminder that life here is in many ways easier, safer, and more prosperous.

The debate in Washington policy circles surrounding the root causes of migration tends to focus on the lack of economic opportunity in Northern Central America. A great deal of attention – and public money – has been devoted to encouraging job-creating investment in the region and to trumpeting investment commitments and the numbers of jobs they will create for people in Northern Central America, as though that is the end of the story.

Gang violence and violence against women are also driving people to seek their fortunes elsewhere. Many programs intended to reduce violence have been in place for decades, and yet the problem has only gotten worse.

Poor governance is a key factor, but one that's notoriously resistant to foreign intervention. Assistance to these imperfect but functioning democracies instead tends to focus on training law enforcement and justice-sector personnel in the hope that the citizenry will one day demand good governance.

All these programs are well intended and, in some cases, actually effective – within a relatively narrow scope. More investment is better than less and creates opportunity. Successfully implemented community policing programs can reduce gang violence in neighborhoods. By strengthening the infrastructure of shelters, survivors of assault can find support and services. And training programs do boost the expertise and effectiveness of law enforcement organizations.

While only Central Americans themselves can resolve the problem of poor governance, there is potential for effective interventions. These interventions must consider the intersection of root causes and the underpinning of poor governance, ultimately encouraging Northern Central Americans to move toward a freer and more prosperous society.

The root causes of migration from Northern Central America

Corruption, a regularly cited problem in Central America, is both a cause and an effect of poor governance. It's easy to name, but difficult to remedy because of its intractable nature. Corruption feeds impunity which feeds inequality which feeds instability which feeds insecurity which weakens institutions which feeds corruption and so on and so forth in an endless cycle.

When corrupt institutions focus primarily on benefiting bureaucrats, they become inefficient and ineffective at achieving their stated goal of serving their people. Everything becomes unreliable. In rural areas, water and electricity may not be available every day. The nearest health centers may be hours away. Schoolteachers don't show up for class, and public hospitals run out of medication.

Weak institutions, meanwhile, have far-reaching impact, such as chronic malnutrition in Guatemalan children, Hondurans averaging only seven years of school, and over 43% of jobs in El Salvador being informal (working for cash, off the books, many times because the employer is not a registered business or is a small street vendor). Chronic malnutrition increases vulnerability to diseases, causes developmental delays, stunts growth, and increases overall rates of infant and child mortality. Economic growth and workforce participation suffer when the number of years of formal schooling completed is low. Informal-sector jobs are typically low wage, with little to no access to social security. They also reduces the amount of tax revenue that governments collect, limiting the availability of funding for social and government services.

When judicial institutions such as the police and courts become corrupt, inefficient, and weak, citizen security is directly affected. **Impunity** becomes widespread, destabilizing communities as there are no legal consequences for crime. In all three countries, over 95% of crimes against women and girls go unpunished. This includes all crimes on the continuum of violence up to sexual assault and femicide. Often referred to as **gender-based violence**, it undermines women and girls' agency and well-being, as well as the stability and prosperity of their communities.

Insecurity is further compounded by the presence of transnational criminal organizations using all three countries as transit routes for the illicit smuggling of people and illegal substances. Local gangs, known as maras, assume control over their self-professed territory – leaving citizens in that area under the control of the gangs and completely unprotected by the state. The presence and prevalence of private security hired by those with above-average resources point to the governments' unwillingness or inability to provide a basic level of safety for their citizens. These structural challenges coupled with social/ cultural ideas and norms around masculinity, gender, and violence create conditions that become untenable, especially for women and children.

Corruption, weak institutions, high levels of violence and impunity lead to **instability and displacement**. Both men and women are more likely to leave areas where violence against women occurs. Most people and displaced families move to other areas within their home country more than once looking for safety and stability. This constant internal migration further destabilizes communities.

In this environment of corruption, weak institutions, gender-based violence, impunity, instability, and displacement, it is no wonder we see **depressed economies**, low female labor force participation, and constrained job growth. Economic interventions alone cannot adequately address the root causes of this poor economic environment. Weak institutions can compound the impact on economic performance, as they also make it difficult for companies to comply with regulations. Regulations that are expensive, difficult to navigate, and cumbersome reduce the chances of compliance. Add in the likelihood of having to pay a petty bribe at each stop in any regulatory process, and it becomes clear how ineffective institutions suppress the formal employment sector.

Just as the confluence of root causes affects citizens' daily lives, it also impacts the business climate. Local businesses struggle under gang "rents" (extortion payments to the gang in exchange for protection from said gang), compete in a bribery-heavy environment, and see low returns for complying with burdensome regulations. Potential foreign investors see a risk calculus that just doesn't make sense for them, especially due to political and legal instability. If the rule of law is not honored for citizens, foreign investors cannot be confident that their business contracts will be. This is true even though these countries hold enormous potential, including proximity to the United States and Western Hemisphere supply chains, a booming working-age population, and preferential trade regulations under CAFTA-DR, the free-trade agreement between the United States, Costa Rica, El Salvador, Guatemala, Honduras, Nicaragua, and the Dominican Republic.

It's important to note that economic migration is a term sometimes used dismissively, as if the economic push factor is trivial and economic migrants are just looking for better malls. It doesn't adequately convey the severity of the situation in places like Guatemala, where 8-year-olds die from malnutrition weighing 37 pounds; 50% of primary age children are chronically malnourished; and infant, child, and maternal mortality rates are all among the highest in the world.

Democracy is receding globally and experiencing its steepest decline in Latin America. Recent developments in El Salvador, Guatemala, and Honduras point to worrying autocratic shifts – at precisely the moment these countries have the most to gain by collaborating with their democratic neighbors. The incredible opportunity of U.S. investment, foreign assistance, aid, and development is being utterly wasted by the rhetoric of autocrats decrying "foreign regimes" at the same time U.S. officials are calling for increased nearshoring and ally-shoring (making supply chains more resilient by moving them and investment closer to the United States).

Populist autocrats have successfully tapped into citizens' frustrations. Many living in the region have no particular affinity for democracy, because they don't think it's ever delivered for them. About half the population surveyed for the 2021 Americas Barometer report published by the Latin American Public Opinion Project at Vanderbilt University indicated a willingness to forego basic democratic institutions like elections if they could gain better income and reliable access to basic services. Autocrats instinctively seize on this sentiment and gain popularity by simultaneously offering benefits (cash transfers, food programs, computers for schools, COVID-19 vaccines, etc.) while they consolidate power, capture legislative and judicial structures, and oppress civil society, including journalists.

All of this comes at a cost: The financial situation in these countries is tenuous and unable to sustain long-term social spending while driving out foreign investment. What we're seeing is this gamble play out. What happens when the autocrat's house of cards come stumbling down and citizens have traded their freedoms but are not better off for it? This is the ultimate root cause of migration – inadequate and undemocratic governance.

Migration and remittances

Leaving home is the only chance for survival for many people, not a choice. Unfortunately, their options are slim. Most people who choose to migrate to the United States moved within their home country first – understandably trying to make it in a place they still call home, where culture and language are native, and social support may be nearby. But persistent inequalities and the ties between wealth and security mean that many of the displaced only have access to areas with equal or worse security concerns.

The confluence of push and pull factors are important to note here: Virtually everyone knows someone who has made it to the United States and is sending money back to their families

AND someone in the community who has been killed. These vastly different outcomes reveal the starkness of the possible futures many must weigh.

Remittances, money sent home from those working abroad, are easily visible by the market distortions they create. They provide a massive influx of liquidity that flows directly to households, directly relieving poverty. Remittances currently make up 15% of GDP in Guatemala and 24% in both El Salvador and Honduras. But they also trigger an effect eerily similar to one seen in oil-rich developing countries: They shift the economy toward services and consumption and away from producing goods while at the same time bidding up the exchange rate and making a country's exports less competitive in international markets.

The result is that families whose members migrate can pay for things like homes and consumer goods, while families who don't have someone sending remittances are stuck in poverty. This further exacerbates existing inequality and reduces pressure on the state to provide social services. Given the lack of legal pathways available, this push to migrate also generates financial incentives for criminal organizations to smuggle people.

Northern Central Americans who migrate through Mexico toward the United States are vulnerable to coyotes (smugglers), gangs, cartels, and police, groups to which they are vulnerable in their home countries, as well. More than 60% of migrants were exposed to a violent situation in the two years before migrating. Women and children in particular are vulnerable to sexual violence, trafficking, and exploitation along the migratory route to the United States, and many women and girls seek a contraceptive shot at the beginning of their journey. This year, **deaths** at the U.S.-Mexico border have reached a historic high. Migrants do not take this journey lightly – they come because the horrors they face at home are so much worse.

Recommendations

The U.S. government should engage with the governments of the region to ensure that assistance to companies investing in the region is accompanied by serious efforts to address business-climate weaknesses

The root causes of migration push out both investment and citizens. Injecting additional investment into this climate without addressing regulatory and other dysfunctions will not create enduring jobs. On the contrary, the minute U.S. subsidies disappear, so will the jobs. This moment of intense focus on the region – and of heightened interest in Northern Central America as an investment location – creates a unique opportunity to shape the business climate. The United States should not squander it.

The U.S. government, in partnership with nonprofit organizations and other democratic governments, should support civil society, including journalists and human rights defenders

Attacks on civil society and the shrinking of safe spaces for dialogue dim the light that civil society is trying to shine on corruption and human rights violations. It also silences the voices calling for the promotion of democracy and strengthening of democratic institutions and democratic norms. Support includes security, targeted funding, refuge for dissidents, among other strategic initiatives to strengthen democracy.

Congress should pass bipartisan immigration reform that reduces pressure at our border and creates legal pathways for Northern Central American migrant workers to contribute to our prosperity

Every year that goes by without reforming the United States immigration system means a missed opportunity to ensure the future prosperity, vitality, and security of our Nation. Investment in a 21st century approach to border management is a key to reducing pressure on our border.

The U.S. government, in partnership with nonprofit organizations, should improve access to legal counsel and trauma support for women and girls fleeing gender-based violence

Violence against women and children (including gender-based violence) is a particularly insidious symptom of weak institutions and a suppressed civil society. The most vulnerable in a society suffer disproportionately when crime goes unpunished.

Only the pillars of democracy – freedom, accountability, and opportunity – will sustainably reverse the momentum of the vicious cycle triggered by the root causes of migration. Free markets and free people are essential to lasting peace and prosperity.

Migration can ultimately be understood as part displacement and part citizens voting with their feet. Efforts to address the root causes of migration from Northern Central America need to bridge the gap between the root cause and democratic governance. A better business climate leads directly to lower corruption in the private sector, increased investment, more jobs in the formal sector, and increased tax revenue.

More jobs in the formal employment sector can make education more valuable, increasing the overall years in formal schooling. Alongside efforts to strengthen the justice system, reducing impunity and insecurity may ensure that the citizens of Northern Central America feel less pressure to leave. At these first inklings of hope, a robust civil society is important. Reduced migration means reduced remittances and increased pressure on the government to provide social services. Weak institutions and authoritarian leaders will not be keen to change the status quo. Civil society, including journalists, human rights defenders, and democracy promoters will play a key role educating the citizens of Northern Central America of their rights and exposing corruption and corrupt actors. With free and fair elections, leaders can be voted in that more accurately reflect the will of the people.

The global democratic community has a responsibility to support those working tirelessly to change the trajectory toward authoritarianism in their communities. The United States can do this in Northern Central America by taking tangible action, narrow in scope but broad in impact, informed by an understanding of the interconnectedness of the root causes of migration, to disrupt the vicious cycle of corruption, impunity, and authoritarianism. With our support, the citizens of Northern Central America can generate a wave, *una ola*, of not just better circumstances, but of hope.

Although commitment to democracy in the region is at a low point, the citizens of El Salvador, Guatemala, and Honduras ultimately do have the agency to vote for leaders that will uphold democratic norms and institutions and to vote out leaders that don't. By their vote, their voice can be heard, and their governments held accountable.

Periodical and Internet Sources Bibliography

The following articles have been selected to supplement the diverse views presented in this chapter.

Nick Cumming Bruce, "Number of People Fleeing Conflict is Highest Since World War II, U.N. Says," *The New York Times*, June 19, 2019. https://www.nytimes.com/2019/06/19/world/refugees-record-un.html.

Manny Fernandez, "Inside the Former Walmart That is Now a Shelter for Almost 1,500 Migrant Children," *The New York Times*, June 14, 2018. https://www.nytimes.com/2018/06/14/us/family-separation-migrant-children-detention.html.

Chris Fuchs, "New Legislation Introduced to End EB-5 Immigrant Investor Program," NBC News, February 3, 2017. https://www.nbcnews.com/news/asian-america/new-legislation-introduced-end-eb-5-immigrant-investor-program-n716621.

Hannah Hartig, "Republicans turn more negative toward refugees as number admitted to U.S. plummets," Pew Research Center, May 24, 2018. https://www.pewresearch.org/short-reads/2018/05/24/republicans-turn-more-negative-toward-refugees-as-number-admitted-to-u-s-plummets/.

Suzy Khimm, "How long is the immigration 'line'? As long as 24 years," *The Washington Post,* January 31, 2013. https://www.washingtonpost.com/news/wonk/wp/2013/01/31/how-long-is-the-immigration-line-as-long-as-24-years/.

Julia Manchester, "Dem senator shares video of him being barred entry to immigration detention center," The Hill, June 03, 2018. https://thehill.com/homenews/senate/390499-dem-senator-barred-entry-to-immigration-detention-facility/.

Nomaan Merchant, "Hundreds of children wait in Border Patrol facility in Texas," Associated Press, June 18, 2018. https://apnews.com/article/9794de32d39d4c6f89fbefaea3780769.

Alex Nowrasteh, "Illegal Immigrants and Crime – Assessing the Evidence," CATO Institute, March 4, 2019. https://www.cato.org/blog/illegal-immigrants-crime-assessing-evidence.

Jynnah Radfor and Phillip Connor, "Canada now leads the world in refugee resettlement, surpassing the U.S.," Pew Research Center, June 19, 2019. https://www.pewresearch.org/short-reads/2019/06/19/canada-now-leads-the-world-in-refugee-resettlement-surpassing-the-u-s/.

Elana Schor, "Trump administration proposes historically low refugee limit," Associated Press, September 26, 2019. https://apnews.com/article/immigration-donald-trump-united-states-politics-86909101dde746bfb7395bf9f47fda8e.

"US attorney general quotes Bible to defend separating families," BBC News, June 15, 2018. https://www.bbc.com/news/world-us-canada-44499048.

"Why the US is separating migrant children from their parents," BBC News, June 15, 2018. https://www.bbc.com/news/world-us-canada-44503514.

Chapter 4

Are the Current Pathways to Naturalization & Citizenship Sufficient for Today's Needs?

Chapter Preface

One of the most common arguments about undocumented (sometimes called "illegal") immigrants is, "Why don't they just come into the country legally?" or "Why don't they just apply legally for asylum or citizenship?"

The answer to either version of the argument rests upon yet another question: How easy, and how affordable, are the pathways to naturalization and citizenship that are currently available to immigrants?

When one considers how often people are coming to the United States from countries that are torn apart by war or are fleeing poverty, oppression, violence, or other impossible situations, we must acknowledge the fact that many of them are arriving with little more than the clothes on their backs. Therefore, is it really as easy to "follow the law" and enter the country legally as people claim it is?

The viewpoints in this chapter delve into this facet of the immigration debate. They examine how accessible and affordable the current pathways to entry and citizenship are. They ask readers to consider if the current pathways are sufficient to meet the needs of the steady flow of incoming immigrants in both a timely and humane manner.

Readers who carefully consider the viewpoints in this chapter may be surprised by what they learn about the complexities and pitfalls inherent in the system.

Viewpoint 1

> *"Prevention through deterrence is a failed policy with a tragic human cost."*

Trump's Plans for Tougher Border Enforcement Won't Necessarily Stop Migrants

Katrina Burgess

In the following viewpoint, Katrina Burgess discusses why the border policies espoused by President Trump would not be effective at stopping undocumented immigrants from entering the United States. She also explains how the policies would increase the cost and danger for immigrants, and she reminds readers that using undocumented immigrants as scapegoats is not a new distraction method for U.S. lawmakers.

As you read, consider the following questions:

1. According to the author, what are the main reasons the border policies being discussed are unlikely to be effective at stopping undocumented immigration?
2. According to the author, who will reap the most benefits from the border policies in question, and why?

3. What credentials and evidence does the author present to support her position? Do these credentials and evidence seem reliable?

The screen fills with images of migrants dodging highway traffic. "They keep coming," says a narrator. "The federal government won't stop them yet requires us to pay billions to take care of them. … Enough is enough."

This message might sound familiar, but it isn't new. It's a 1994 campaign ad in support of Republican politician Pete Wilson's run for reelection as California governor.

At the time, California was experiencing its worst recession in decades. Although immigrants living in the state illegally did not cause California's economic crisis, they were a convenient scapegoat. By blaming immigrants for California's financial woes, Wilson turned his faltering campaign around and won reelection in November 1994.

Thirty years later, the United States is in a similar political moment, with many Americans worried about the cost of living and immigration.

President-elect Donald Trump has repeatedly – and misleadingly – blamed immigrants for crime, high housing costs and other problems. He is promising to quickly close the U.S. southern border and deport the nearly 12 million immigrants without legal authorization to remain in the country.

As a scholar of migration in the Americas, my research shows that Trump's approach is unlikely to stop migrants from trying to enter the U.S. but very likely to enrich criminals. Migrants will keep fleeing desperate circumstances under even more treacherous conditions that leave them vulnerable to exploitation by criminal groups.

Prevention through deterrence

A few months after Wilson's campaign ad hit the airwaves, the U.S. Border Patrol issued its strategic plan for 1994 and beyond.

In this plan, the Border Patrol proposed a strategy called "prevention through deterrence" that was designed to make illegal entry across the southwest land border so risky that potential migrants would decide to stay home.

By concentrating border enforcement in the urban areas where most migrants were trying to cross, the plan aimed to force them "over more hostile terrain" in the desert and to increase the cost of hiring a smuggler.

Today, illegal migration to the U.S. is far more deadly and expensive than it was 30 years ago, just as the authors of the 1994 Border Patrol plan anticipated.

But the report's authors believed that potential migrants would forgo the dangers of migrating to the U.S. without authorization, as well as the high costs of getting there. They thought potential migrants would simply stay in their home countries.

They were wrong.

Fortified borders

The strategy of discouraging migrants from coming to the U.S. by making it more difficult required a large federal investment in border enforcement and cooperation from other countries, especially Mexico.

Over the past 30 years, the Border Patrol's budget has grown more than sevenfold, and the number of agents stationed along the southwest border has quadrupled.

The U.S. government has also built physical infrastructure to stop migrants from entering the country, including massive walls that extend into the Pacific Ocean.

In more remote areas, drones, surveillance towers and extreme temperatures do the work of border control, often with deadly consequences for migrants.

The U.S. also provided more than $176 million in funding between October 2014 and Sept. 30, 2023, to support Mexico's immigration control efforts.

There is some evidence that stricter border enforcement deterred Mexicans from crossing illegally into the United States after the 1990s. The number of migrants apprehended by the Border Patrol along the southwest border plummeted from 1.6 million between October 1999 through the end of September 2000, to 327,577 between October 2010 and the end of September 2011.

But the deterrent effect of increased enforcement did not last. Migrant apprehensions at the southwest border began to rise again in 2012 and spiked to 851,508 between October 2018 and Sept. 30, 2019. After falling briefly during the pandemic, total apprehensions averaged 1.9 million per year between October 2020 and Sept. 30, 2024.

These numbers exceed the historic peaks in 1986 and 2000 – despite the much greater costs and dangers of migrating illegally today.

Illusory deterrence

In 2023, my research team and I interviewed over 130 migrants in Colombia, Costa Rica and Mexico to understand why they were taking such enormous risks to get to the United States. What we found is that deterrence isn't working because of shifts in who is migrating and why they are leaving home.

Until 2011, the vast majority of illegal border crossers were Mexicans, mostly young men seeking higher incomes to support their families. As the Mexican economy recovered and fewer young people entered the labor market, Mexican workers had less need to migrate. Those who made it to the United States stayed put instead of going back and forth.

Today, more than 60% of the migrants who cross the U.S. border without legal authorization are from places other than Mexico, including Central America, Venezuela, Ecuador and Haiti. Forty percent of them are parents traveling with children.

Many of these migrants are fleeing chronic violence, rampant corruption, natural disasters or economic collapse.

For these migrants, it is worth the risk of being kidnapped, dying in the desert or being deported to escape a desperate situation.

"If they deport me, sister, I will come back," a Honduran mother of three told us in Tijuana in June 2023. "If you go back, you die. So you have to go forward, forward, forward all the time."

Increased criminality

While prevention through deterrence has not stopped migrants, it has enriched smugglers, corrupt government officials and other criminals who take advantage of vulnerable migrants on their way to the U.S. border.

"Before I would charge you $6,000," explained a Salvadoran smuggler to an Associated Press reporter in December 2019. "Now I am charging you double. And depending on the obstacles on the way, the price can go up."

This doesn't include the fee to cross the heavily fortified U.S.-Mexico border, which increased from a few hundred dollars in the 1990s to between $2,000 and $15,000 today.

According to one estimate, smuggling revenues in the Americas grew from $500 million in 2018 to $13 billion in 2022. "Criminals have shifted from their primary business, which was drug trafficking," the director of an anti-kidnapping unit at an attorney general's office in Chihuahua, Mexico, told a journalist in June 2024. "Now 60 to 70% of their focus is migrant smuggling."

It's not just smuggling that is lucrative. As Mexico's own immigration policy has become more restrictive, migrants have fallen into the clutches of an extensive extortion racket that involves kidnapping migrants once they set foot in Mexico.

Prevention through deterrence is a failed policy with a tragic human cost. It doesn't stop migrants who are fleeing dire conditions, and it fuels violence and criminality. Drug cartels, armed groups and corrupt officials get rich while insecurity spreads, fueling more migration. It is a vicious cycle that will likely only get worse with stricter enforcement and mass deportations.

Viewpoint 2

> *"Among Democrats and Republicans, there are areas of ideological agreement – and some notable differences – on the severity of problems in the U.S."*

How Americans View Immigration and Other Issues

Pew Research Center

In this report, the Pew Research Center discusses opposing views of the major issues facing the United States ahead of the 2020 presidential campaign and election season, including such topics as immigration, climate change, and health care. The report also delves into the main reasons differing views exist on these topics. Although this research was conducted in the recent past, it still reveals helpful information about the views of the American public.

As you read, consider the following questions:

1. Why do you think immigration falls where it does on the list of issues Americans are concerned about? Do you think it would fall in a different place on the list today?
2. How does the data presented align with your own concerns?

"1. Views of the major problems facing the country". Pew Research Center, Washington, D.C (December 17, 2019) https://www.pewresearch.org/politics/2019/12/17/views-of-the-major-problems-facing-the-country/

3. How do the statistics presented here reflect the political and ideological divisions currently found in the United States?

When asked to consider the major problems facing the country, the affordability of health care and drug addiction top the American public's list.

Other issues, including illegal immigration and climate change, are seen as less pressing, due in part to stark partisan disagreements over the importance of these issues.

Two-thirds of Americans view the affordability of health care as a very big problem for the country today, while another 26% say it is a moderately big problem. Fewer than one-in-ten say affording health care is a small problem (6%) or not a problem at all (2%).

A comparable majority says drug addiction is a major problem: 64% say it is a very big problem in the country and 28% say it is a moderately big problem.

Narrower majorities say the affordability of a college education (55%) and the federal budget deficit (53%) are very big problems in the country. About half say this about climate change (48%).

Somewhat smaller shares of the public cite other issues as very big problems for the country. For instance, 43% say this about illegal immigration and 39% say this about terrorism.

Sexism and job opportunities rank at the bottom of the public's list of problems in the country. At a time when the public holds positive views of the economy overall, just 25% say job opportunities for all Americans is a very big problem. About the same share (26%) calls sexism a very big problem.

For the most part, assessments of the pressing problems facing the U.S. have not changed a great deal in recent years. However, the shares of Americans who say that terrorism and job opportunities for all Americans are very big problems have declined substantially since November 2016, shortly before the presidential election. At that time, 53% viewed terrorism as a very big problem; today, 39% express this view. And the share who view job opportunities as a very big problem is only about half the level it was three years ago (25% now, 47% then).

Wide partisan differences in views of most major problems

As in the past, there are wide partisan differences on the perceived seriousness of most of the problems asked about in the survey. Democrats and Democratic-leaning independents are far more likely than Republicans and GOP leaners to say several concerns are very big problems – especially climate change, economic inequality and racism.

Majorities of Democrats say all three are very big problems, compared with fewer than a quarter of Republicans. For example, 73% of Democrats say climate change is a very big problem, compared with just 17% of Republicans. (For more on partisanship and views of climate change, see "U.S. Public Views on Climate and Energy.")

Republicans, by contrast, are more likely to say illegal immigration is a very big problem. Two-thirds of Republicans say illegal immigration is a very big problem; the only problem cited by similar shares of Republicans is drug addiction (68%). Just 23% of Democrats cite illegal immigration as a very big problem, the lowest share for any of the 11 issues included in the survey.

There are a handful of issues that are viewed similarly across partisan lines: Majorities in both parties say drug addiction is a very big problem, though Republicans are more likely than Democrats to express this view (68% vs. 61%). About half of Republicans (54%) and Democrats (52%) say the federal budget deficit is a very big problem. Terrorism ranks relatively low as a concern among Republicans (41%) and Democrats (36%).

Among Democrats and Republicans, there are areas of ideological agreement – and some notable differences – on the severity of problems in the U.S.

On climate change, liberal Democrats (84%) are significantly more likely than conservative and moderate Democrats (64%)

to say this is a very big problem. Among Republicans, 28% of moderates and liberals say climate change is a very big problem compared with an even smaller share of conservatives (11%).

Illegal immigration is the top national problem among conservative Republicans (75% say it is a very big problem), but is viewed as a major problem by fewer moderate and liberal Republicans (53%). Conservative and moderate Democrats are twice as likely as liberal Democrats to say illegal immigration is a very big problem (30% vs. 15%).

Notably, one national concern – drug addiction – is viewed as a very big problem by majorities across the ideological spectrum. Two-thirds of conservative and moderate Democrats (66%) say drug addiction is a very big problem; a smaller majority of liberal Democrats (57%) say the same. Nearly identical shares of conservative Republicans (68%) and moderate and liberal Republicans (66%) say drug addiction is a very big problem.

Age differences in views of the nation's biggest problems

In views of several national problems, the age differences are fairly modest. For example, comparable majorities across age categories say the affordability of health care is a very big problem.

Yet there are notable age differences on such issues as illegal immigration, the federal budget deficit, terrorism and climate change.

On three of these four issues – illegal immigration, the deficit and terrorism – older adults are more likely than young people to regard them as very big problems. For example, 57% of those ages 65 and older and nearly as many ages 50 to 64 (53%) view illegal immigration as a major problem. Fewer than half of those ages 30 to 49 (38%) and only about a quarter of those younger than 30 (23%) say the same.

By contrast, adults under age 30 are the only age group in which a majority (59%) views climate change as a very big problem.

Smaller shares of those 30 to 49 (47%), 50 to 64 (42%) and 65 and older (44%) place the same level of importance on the issue.

While there are sizable age differences in views of some national problems, these differences are far more pronounced among Republicans and Republican leaners than Democrats and Democratic leaners.

The most striking age gap, by far, in opinions among Republicans is on illegal immigration: Republicans ages 65 and older are 50 percentage points more likely than those younger than 30 to say illegal immigration is a very big problem for the country (85% vs. 35%).

The youngest Republicans also are less likely than older adults in the GOP to say terrorism and the federal budget deficit are very big problems for the country.

On climate change, the age pattern among Republicans runs in the opposite direction. Just 15% of Republicans ages 30 and older say climate change is a very big problem for the country. The youngest Republicans are more likely to see the issue as a very big problem; still, the overall share of young Republicans who say this is relatively modest (32%).

Views of top problems vary by race and ethnicity

Views of the country's most pressing problems also differ by race and ethnicity. In general, black and Hispanic adults tend to be more likely than whites to assign high importance to a range of issues.

One of the largest divides in views is over the issue of racism. Majorities of blacks (75%) and Hispanics (61%) view racism as a very big problem in the country today. By contrast, just 33% of whites give the issue the same level of importance.

Two-thirds of blacks (66%) view economic inequality as a very big problem for the country; 51% of Hispanics share this view. Among whites, 39% view economic inequality as a very big problem.

When it comes to job opportunities for all Americans, 53% of black adults say this is a very big problem for the country today, compared with smaller shares of Hispanics (31%) and whites (18%).

Democrats differ by race and ethnicity in their views of some of the major problems in the country. (Differences by race and ethnicity among Republicans were not analyzed due to insufficient sample sizes. Most Republicans and Republican leaners are white; the share of nonwhites in the GOP is far smaller than among Democrats.)

Among Democrats and Democratic leaners, 52% of whites say racism is a very big problem for the country, compared with larger shares of black (79%) and Hispanic (70%) Democrats.

White Democrats are ideologically divided on this issue: While a 60% majority of white liberals say racism is a very big problem, just 41% of white conservative and moderate Democrats say the same.

In addition, black Democrats (52%) are more likely than white (25%) or Hispanic Democrats (37%) to view job opportunities for all Americans as a very big problem.

Economic inequality is viewed as a major problem by nearly identical shares of black and white Democrats (70% and 68% respectively); a somewhat smaller majority of Hispanic Democrats (59%) view inequality as a very big problem. Yet there are wide ideological differences among white Democrats: 78% of white liberals see inequality as a very big problem, compared with 56% of white conservative and moderate Democrats.

Climate change divides Democrats by race and ethnicity, and white Democrats by ideology. Among white and Hispanic Democrats, roughly as many cite climate change as a very big problem for the country as cite the affordability of health care. Among black Democrats, however, 56% say climate change is a very big problem, compared with 79% who say the affordability of health care is a major problem.

Among white Democrats, an overwhelming share of liberals (89%) say climate change is a very big problem for the country. A smaller majority of white conservative and moderate Democrats (69%) say climate change is a major problem for the U.S.

VIEWPOINT 3

> *"Overall though, lessons from the Age of Mass Migration suggest that fears immigrants can't fit into American society are misplaced."*

What History Tells Us About the Assimilation of Immigrants

Ran Abramitzky

In the following viewpoint, Ran Abramitzky presents historical context surrounding the ability of new immigrants to assimilate into American culture. This context is based on research performed by Abramitzky, Leah Boustan of UCLA, and Katherine Eriksson of UC Davis. They reviewed data about the occupations of immigrants who arrived during the Age of Mass Migration (1850-1913), challenging the largely-held belief that most immigrants arrived penniless and worked low-paying jobs in order to succeed. They discuss the difficulty surrounding the collection of cultural data and how they adjusted their methodology to account for this. They finally present conclusions as to the effectiveness of forced assimilation when compared with naturally-occurring assimilation, and what this could mean for future immigration policies.

"What History Tells Us about Assimilation of Immigrants" by Ran Abramitzky, Stanford University, April, 2017. Reprinted by Permission.

As you read, consider the following questions:

1. Why is it important to consider the historical data surrounding immigrant assimilation when considering how to reshape current immigration policies?
2. What factors did the author and their research partners consider when examining the data in context, and how does this affect the conclusions they make overall?
3. What conclusions can you make, based on the information presented, about the importance of assimilation to immigrants' ability to succeed in the United States?

Immigration has emerged as a decisive — and sharply divisive — issue in the United States. Skepticism about whether new arrivals can assimilate into American society was a key concern in the 2016 presidential election and remains an ongoing theme in the public debate on immigration policy. This controversy is not new. The U.S. has experienced repeated waves of hostility toward immigrants and today's concerns echo alarms sounded often in the past. Both today and in earlier times, many in this country have viewed immigrants as a threat to the integrity of the nation's culture, fearing that foreigners among us somehow make America less American. Consider the following statement: Immigration "is bringing to the country people whom it is very difficult to assimilate and who do not promise well for the standard of civilization in the United States." The speaker was not Donald Trump on the campaign trail but Massachusetts Sen. Henry Cabot Lodge in 1891.

The immigration debate raises a fundamental issue: Are immigrants able to successfully integrate into American society by adopting the economic, social, and cultural norms of native-born Americans? Or are they likely to remain an alien presence inside our borders long after they settle here? This argument typically generates more heat than light. Many people have opinions on the subject, but relatively little empirical evidence is available on how fully and quickly immigrants assimilate into U.S. culture.

Leah Boustan of UCLA, Katherine Eriksson of UC Davis, and I have tried to fill part of this gap by looking at immigration during the Age of Mass Migration from 1850 to 1913, when U.S. borders were open and 30 million Europeans picked up stakes to move here. By the early 20th century, some 15 percent of the U.S. population was foreign born, comparable to the share today. If we want to know how today's newcomers will fare, we can find important clues by examining what happened to those who arrived on our shores during the greatest surge of immigration in U.S. history.

In our previous work on immigration, my co-authors and I looked at occupation data of immigrants who arrived during the Age of Mass Migration.[1] The classic narrative is that penniless immigrants worked low-paying jobs to pull themselves up by their bootstraps, eventually reaching equality of skills and income with natives. We found that story to be largely a myth. On average, long-term immigrants and natives held jobs at similar skill levels and climbed the occupational ladder at about the same pace. We did find considerable variation though. Immigrants from richer countries, such as England or Germany, often worked in higher-skilled occupations than natives, while those from poorer countries, such as Italy or Russia, often were in less-skilled occupations. But, regardless of the starting point, the initial gaps between immigrants and natives persisted throughout their lives. These findings provide useful data on the experiences of immigrants in the U.S. labor market. But it's important to stress that even immigrants who lag economically may successfully assimilate into American society.

Measuring cultural assimilation is a challenge because data on cultural practices—things like food, dress, and accent—are not systematically collected. But the names that parents choose for their children are collected, offering a revealing window into the cultural assimilation process.[2] Using 2 million census records from 1920 and 1940, we constructed a foreignness index indicating the probability that a given name would be held by a foreigner or a native.

For example, people with names like Hyman or Vito were almost certain to be children of immigrants, while youngsters with names like Clay or Lowell were likely to have native parents. In this respect, children's names are signals of cultural identity. Giving a child an American-sounding name is a financially cost-free way of identifying with U.S. culture. Thus, we can trace the assimilation process by examining changes in the names immigrants gave their offspring as they spent more time in the U.S.

Our key finding is that for immigrants who arrived in the 1900s and 1910s, the more time they spent in the U.S., the less likely they were to give their children foreign-sounding names. Figure 1 shows that after 20 years in this country, half of the gap in name choice between immigrants and natives had disappeared. The shift in name choice happened at a roughly equal pace for sons and daughters and among poor and rich families.

However, the pace varied significantly depending on country of origin. Immigrants from Norway, Sweden, and Denmark were among the quickest to adopt American-sounding names, followed by Italians and other Southern Europeans. Russians, including

Figure 1.

Immigrants selected less foreign names for children after spending time in US, (Dependent variable = F-index)

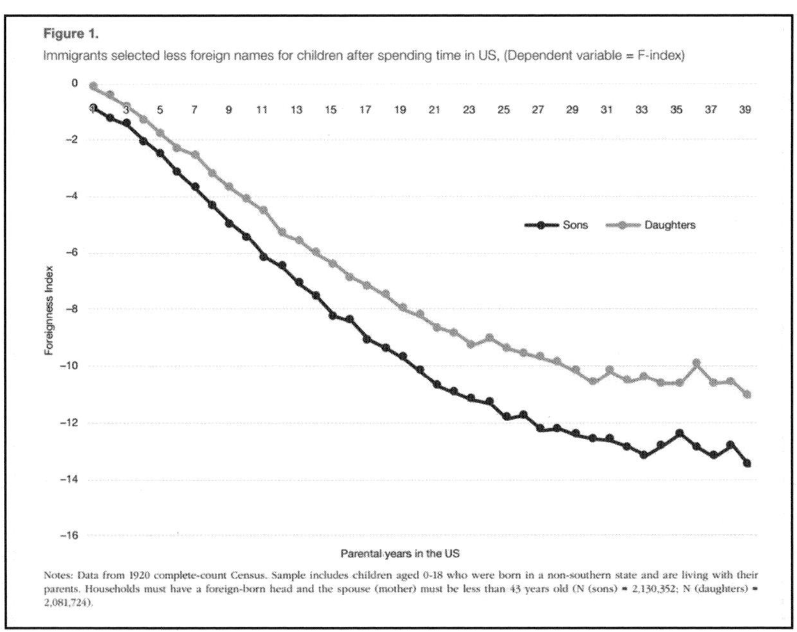

Notes: Data from 1920 complete-count Census. Sample includes children aged 0-18 who were born in a non-southern state and are living with their parents. Households must have a foreign-born head and the spouse (mother) must be less than 43 years old (N (sons) = 2,130,352; N (daughters) = 2,081,724).

many Russian Jews, and Finns had the slowest rates of name-based assimilation. This convergence of names chosen by immigrant and native populations is suggestive evidence of cultural assimilation. But the fact that immigrants didn't fully adopt native naming patterns suggests that many valued retaining a distinct cultural identity.

Having an American-sounding name was a badge of assimilation that conferred genuine economic and social benefits. We looked at census records of more than a million children of immigrants from 1920, when they lived with their childhood families, through 1940, when they were adults.

Children with less-foreign-sounding names completed more years of schooling, earned more, and were less likely to be unemployed than their counterparts whose names sounded more foreign. In addition, they were less likely to marry someone born abroad or with a foreign-sounding name. These patterns held even among brothers within the same family. The data suggest that, while a foreign-sounding name reinforced a sense of ethnic identity, it may have exposed individuals to discrimination at school or on the job.

Other measures reinforce the picture of early 20th century immigrants gradually taking on American cultural markers. By 1930, more than two-thirds of immigrants had applied for citizenship and almost all reported they could speak some English. A third of first-generation immigrants who arrived unmarried and more than half of second-generation immigrants wed spouses from outside their cultural group.

These findings suggest that over time immigrants' sense of separateness weakened and their identification with U.S. culture grew stronger. The gradual adoption of American-sounding names appears to have been part of a process of assimilation in which newcomers learned U.S. culture, made a commitment to build roots in this country, and came to identify as Americans.

Some may have arrived with a strong desire to assimilate, but little knowledge of how to do so. They may not even have known which names were common in the U.S. Others may not have cared about assimilating at first, but eventually felt the urge to blend in.

In both cases, as time went by, they may have started to navigate the dominant culture with greater ease. Their children may have attended schools with children from other cultures and have spoken with American accents.

What does this tell us about the assimilation process? We can imagine that after many years in the U.S., immigrants, like natives, become baseball fans, eat hamburgers, and watch fireworks on the Fourth of July. To be sure, their connections with their countries of origin are not obliterated. Instead, they may come to see themselves as hyphenated Americans, but Americans nonetheless.

What's more, policies that attempt to force cultural assimilation on immigrants may backlash. Fouka (2015) finds that German immigrants in states that introduced anti-German language policies during World War I responded by choosing visibly German names, perhaps as a show of community support.**[3]**

Concerns about the economic effects of immigration go hand in hand with fears that immigrants will remain a culturally foreign presence in our midst. How immigration affects the income and living standards of natives and how newcomers contribute to the U.S. economy are hot-button issues. My research partners and I are in the process of investigating these questions. Based on the existing literature and our own research, we hypothesize that the economic impact of immigration today may be different from the effects during the Age of Mass Migration.**[4]** In the early 20th century, foreign-born and native workers competed for the same low-skilled jobs and immigrants may have driven down wages of those born here. Today, the competition between immigrants and natives may be less important because immigrants tend to cluster in a limited set of occupations at the top and bottom of income distribution.

The historical evidence presented here should be considered with care. Today's immigrants differ markedly in ethnicity, education, and occupation from those who came during the Age of Mass Migration. Over the past half century, the U.S. has experienced a second wave of mass migration with characteristics that set it apart from what took place in the late 19th and early 20th centuries.

The contemporary migration wave is highly regulated, favoring those with money, education, and skills and drawing migrants primarily from Asia and Latin America. Selection of immigrants today is often positive, meaning those who come here are more highly skilled than their compatriots who stay in their countries of origin. In the past, immigrants were sometimes negatively selected, meaning they were less skilled than those who stayed behind. Finally, legal immigration now is accompanied by a large undocumented inflow, which complicates efforts to study immigration effects.

Much work remains to be done to understand the cultural and economic dimensions of immigration and the differences between the past and the present. My research colleagues and I recently got access to California birth certificate records, which will allow us to compare immigrants from current and historical periods to see whether assimilation patterns are similar.

Overall though, lessons from the Age of Mass Migration suggest that fears immigrants can't fit into American society are misplaced. It would be a mistake to determine our nation's immigration policy based on the belief that immigrants will remain foreigners, preserving their old ways of life and keeping themselves at arm's length from the dominant culture. The evidence is clear that assimilation is real and measurable, that over time immigrant populations come to resemble natives, and that new generations form distinct identities as Americans.

Footnotes

[1] Ran Abramitzky, Leah Platt Boustan, and Katherine Eriksson. (2014). "A Nation of Immigrants: Assimilation and Economic Outcomes in the Age of Mass Migration." Journal of Political Economy. 122(3): 467-506.

[2] Ran Abramitzky, Leah Platt Boustan, and Katherine Eriksson. (2016). "Cultural Assimilation During the Age of Mass Migration." Working paper, and references therein.

[3] Vasiliki Fouka. (2015). "Backlash: The Unintended Effects of Language Prohibition in U.S. Schools after World War I." Manuscript.

[4]Ran Abramitzky, and Leah Platt Boustan. (2016a). "Immigration in American Economic History." NBER Working Paper No. 21882, and references therein.]

Viewpoint 4

> *"Title 42 was a justification to oppress marginalised populations, such as immigrants, those living in poverty, women, and people of colour, and denying access to human rights of immigrants and asylum seekers."*

Asylum Seekers Need to be Treated Under Civil Rights Laws

National Library of Medicine

In the following viewpoint, researchers from the National Library of Medicine present the argument that people who arrive in the United States seeking asylum need to be treated according to U.S. civil rights laws. They discuss the importance of the UN's Universal Declaration of Human Rights, and how this should govern the way asylum seekers are dealt with. They address how different presidential administrations have dealt with immigrants and asylum seekers in recent years, and make suggestions for how policies should be changed moving forward.

As you read, consider the following questions:

1. What data does the National Library of Medicine present in support of their claims, and does that data appear to be from unbiased, reliable sources?

2. According to the article, how did the COVID-19 pandemic affect the treatment of asylum seekers specifically, and immigrants in general, in the U.S.?
3. Why is the UN's Declaration of Human Rights integral to this issue?

The United Nations Universal Declaration of Human Rights states that, "everyone has the right to seek and to enjoy in other countries asylum from persecution". Latin Americans from several countries (ie Mexico, Guatemala, Honduras) seek asylum in the USA, looking for protection, security, and a way to provide for their families. Those who seek asylum must provide evidence that they meet the definition of a refugee. Despite the declaration of Human Rights, the civil rights of immigrants in the USA have continued to be violated. The denouncement of an e-mail stating that migrant children were being pushed into the Rio Grande river by Texas troopers, a girl dying after being denied medical care, and the installation of a floating barrier by the state of Texas to stop people from swimming to cross the border at the Rio Grande river confirm that the violence against immigrants is far from over, once again crossing the line of basic human rights. Despite the termination of Title 42, the immigration policy implemented during President Trump's administration that allowed the removal of migrants crossing the USA–Mexico border, President Biden's restrictions on asylum seekers are still very strict and invite the question of whether his statement on humane treatment and civil rights for immigrants will actually be enforced.

At the beginning of the COVID-19 pandemic, Title 42 was implemented as a public health measure that allowed US authorities to expel migrants, including asylum seekers, at the US border. Title 42 was a controversial act ordered by the US Centers for Disease Control and Prevention, without scientific evidence supposed to protect people from being infected by COVID-19. As pointed out by Ulrich and Crosby, Title 42 was a justification to oppress marginalised populations, such as immigrants, those living in poverty, women, and people of colour, and denying access to human rights of immigrants and asylum seekers. More than 13,480 reports of violent conduct, including murder, torture, and kidnapping, have been reported since President Biden took office on Jan 20, 2021. Although COVID-19 cases dropped in most countries months before, Title 42 was only terminated on May 11, 2023, days after the declaration by WHO about the end of the global health emergency. With the termination of Title 42, President Biden proposed a rule to deny asylum to migrants at the USA–Mexico border, which was blocked by judge Jon Tigar from California.

The new restrictions present challenges for people seeking asylum, as those who enter the USA between legal border crossings are considered ineligible. Thus, people who do not request protection in transit countries, such as Mexico, or cross between ports of entry, are disqualified from claiming asylum and denied re-entrance to the USA for 5 years. Asylum seekers must wait in Mexico and are required to wait for their immigration court hearings that can last more than a year. Over the past 15 years, the number of border patrol arrests have increased greatly and, as discussed by Cameron and colleagues, families must stay in shelters that pose risks for their health due to overcrowding, poor sanitation, and precarious infrastructure. Violence against women has also been reported, with high rates of rape and feminicide by people involved in organised crime and by USA and Mexican officers. Children suffer with lack of education and family separation, which have huge impacts on their mental health and increasing risk for post-traumatic disorder.

For the children that eventually cross the border, the Deferred Action for Childhood Arrivals programme (DACA), that provided work authorisation and deportation protection for those who entered in the USA as children is no longer an option. In October, 2022, the DACA programme was put on hold on the basis that it was unlawful, preventing new applications and creating speculation about its termination. The programme, implemented by President Obama in 2012, created new opportunities for more than 800,000 children since its start. Although not providing citizenship, one of its benefits was access to employer-sponsored and state-funded health insurance in certain states. One of President Trump's main goals was to terminate DACA and, although this attempt was blocked by the Supreme Court, the decision to stop new applications has shown how the programme's fragility. However, President Biden is trying to increase Medicaid and ACA health coverage to those under DACA. In a thoughtful and provocative viewpoint, Park and colleagues presented some possible paths for continuity of care of migrant population in the USA, such as state-level policymaking to expand coverage to all residents despite their migration status, and expanding health insurance eligibility for undocumented migrants.

As thousands of people arrive at the USA border requesting asylum, it is only fair that they are treated with the same dignity as any other person. They are vulnerable members of society that have suffered persecution and trauma and their rights must be guaranteed. With the termination of Title 42, the USA is in a position that could be decisive for anyone seeking to immigrate to the country. Immigrants are crucial components of American society and contribute to the economy and industry as, among other things, workers and tax payers. Undocumented immigrants do not increase violent crime rates, present lower incarceration rates than those born in the USA, and are less likely to be arrested for homicide. It is up to President Biden to decide if the USA will take a step in the right direction to guarantee proper rights for all those that seek asylum. Title 42 showed the consequences of major actions within the migrant population, having a huge impact on the mental health and long-term development of both adults and children. It is time now to reconcile and provide proper support and resources for migrants to the USA.

Periodical and Internet Sources Bibliography

The following articles have been selected to supplement the diverse views presented in this chapter.

"Asylum in the United States," American Immigration Council, May 9, 2025. https://www.americanimmigrationcouncil.org/fact-sheet/asylum-united-states/.

"Immigrants in the United States," American Immigration Council, September 21, 2021. https://www.americanimmigrationcouncil.org/fact-sheet/immigrants-in-the-united-states/.

Claire Klobucista and Diana Roy, "U.S. Temporary Foreign Worker Visa Programs," Council on Foreign Relations, June 8, 2023. https://www.cfr.org/backgrounder/us-temporary-foreign-worker-visa-programs.

Julia Neusner, Kennji Kizuka, and Eleanor Acer, "Evasion of Asylum Law and Title 42 Abuse Must End – and Never Be Revived," Human Rights First, December 15, 2022. https://humanrightsfirst.org/library/human-rights-stain-public-health-farce/.

Gloria Oladipo, "Texas trooper says they were told to push children into Rio Grande and deny migrants water," *The Guardian,* July 19, 2023. https://www.theguardian.com/us-news/2023/jul/18/texas-troopers-inhumane-migrants-greg-abbott-border-initiative.

Jin K. Park, Stephen Yale-Loehr, and Gunisha Kaur, "DACA, public health, and immigrant restrictions on healthcare in the United States," The Lancet Regional Health - Americas, April 17, 2023. https://www.thelancet.com/action/showPdf?pii=S2667-193X%2823%2900067-4.

Diana Roy, "How the U.S. Asylum Process Works," Council on Foreign Relations, February 19, 2025. https://www.cfr.org/backgrounder/how-us-asylum-process-works.

Emma Stirling-Cameron, Nicole Elizabeth Ramos, and Shira M. Goldenberg, "Deterrence-based asylum policies exacerbate health inequities among women and children seeing safety at the US-Mexico border," The Lancet Regional Health – Americas, August 2023. https://www.thelancet.com/journals/lanam/article/PIIS2667-193X(23)00119-9/fulltext.

Michael R. Ulrich and Sondra S. Crosby, "Title 42, asylum, and politicizing public health," The Lancet Regional Health – Americas, March 2022. https://www.thelancet.com/journals/lanam/article/PIIS2667-193X(21)00120-4/fulltext.

"The Universal Declaration of Human Rights," United Nations, December 10, 1948. https://www.un.org/en/about-us/universal-declaration-of-human-rights.

"We need to talk about migrant minors' health," The Lancet Regional Health – Americas, November 2021. https://www.thelancet.com/journals/lanam/article/PIIS2667-193X(21)00121-6/fulltext.

Nadine Yousif, "Migrant girl death in US custody was 'preventable,'" BBC News, July 19, 2023. https://www.bbc.com/news/world-us-canada-66244304.

For Further Discussion

Chapter 1

1. How do the sentiments presented in Emma Lazarus's "The New Colossus" provide a contrast to current opinions about immigration in the United States? After reading the rest of the viewpoints in Chapter 1, do you think Lazarus's perspective is an unrealistic ideal that cannot be achieved or a goal Americans should be striving to uphold as a country?
2. After reading the viewpoints in this chapter, do you believe that the United States should have a reputation for being a "nation of immigrants"?
3. Based on the information presented in Chapter 1, what conclusion can you make regarding the actual prevalence of undocumented immigration in the United States?

Chapter 2

1. Several of the viewpoints in Chapter 2 discussed the impact that immigration has on the U.S. economy and debt. Why are economic points such important ones when discussing policy debates?
2. Based upon the information presented in this chapter about the rate of criminal activity among documented and undocumented immigrants, what conclusion can you come to about the validity of claims that the majority of undocumented immigrants are criminals?
3. After considering all the viewpoints in this chapter, do you think the United States should be approaching the immigration question from a humanitarian standpoint or an economic one?

Chapter 3

1. After reading Viewpoint 1, do you believe the U.S. has a legal or moral (or both) obligation to accept refugees? Why or why not?
2. Several viewpoints in this chapter make the general argument that some immigration policies in recent years are really xenophobia and racism disguised as "protecting national security." Do you agree or disagree with this perspective, and why?
3. Based on the viewpoints presented in this chapter, is the immigration issue something that must be dealt with locally (state by state), federally (country-wide), or globally? If it is a global issue, it is reasonable to expect the United States to conform to what is decided globally?

Chapter 4

1. After considering the viewpoints in this chapter, do you think it is reasonable to set a time limit for immigrants to assimilate into "American" culture? Why or why not?
2. Do you think the current available pathways to naturalization and citizenship are sufficient for today's needs? If you had the power to do so, what policies would you change in order to address the issue?
3. Why do you think immigration is such a major issue for politicians to discuss?

Organizations to Contact

The editors have compiled the following list of organizations concerned with the issues debated in this book. The descriptions are derived from materials provided by the organizations. All have publications or information available for interested readers. The list was compiled on the date of publication of the present volume; the information provided here may change. Be aware that many organizations take several weeks or longer to respond to inquiries, so allow as much time as possible.

American Immigration Council (AIC)

PMB2026
2001 L Street N.W., Suite 500
Washington, DC 20036
202-507-7500
info@immcouncil.org
www.americanimmigrationcouncil.org

The AIC is an organization that envisions a nation where immigrants are embraced, communities are enriched, and justice prevails for all. They strive to create a society that values immigrants as vital contributors and where everyone is afforded an equal opportunity to thrive socially, economically, and culturally.

Amnesty International – Americas International Secretariat Office

Calle Luz Savinon
519 Colonia del Valle,
Benito Juarez, 03100, Ciudad de Mexico
Mexico
amnesty.org

Amnesty International is a global movement of more than 10 million people who are committed to creating a future where human rights are enjoyed by everyone. They are independent of any political ideology, economic interest, or religion. They stand with victims of human rights violations, whoever they are, wherever they are.

CATO Institute

1000 Massachusetts Avenue NW
Washington, DC 2000-5403
202-842-0200
www.cato.org

The CATO Institute is an independent organization dedicated to principles and values instead of politics and partisanship. On its website, you can read their blog and articles, listen to podcasts, watch video clips, and sign up for a newsletter.

Council on Foreign Relations

58 East 68th Street
New York, NY 10065
212-434-9400
www.cfr.org

The Council on Foreign Relations is an independent nonpartisan organization and think tank which promotes discussion of pressing issues facing the United States and the world. It hosts the Center for Preventative Action which has information about the issues of hate speech and hate groups.

Human Rights First

121 W 36th Street
PMB 520
New York, NY 10018
212-845-5200
humanrightsfirst.org

Established in 1978, Human Rights First's mission is to ensure that the United States is a global leader on human rights. The organization works in the United States and abroad to promote respect for human rights and the rule of law.

The Leadership Conference

1620 L Street NW
Suite 1100
Washington, DC 20036
202-466-3311
civilrights.org

Since 1950, the Leadership Conference has tirelessly worked for civil rights and social justice. This site includes resources to support the rights of individuals including action against hate and bias.

Migration Policy Institute

1275 K Street NW
Suite 800
Washington, DC 20005
202-266-1940
info@migrationpolicy.org
www.migrationpolicy.org

The Migration Policy Institute is an independent, nonpartisan think tank that seeks to improve immigration and integration policies through authoritative research and analysis, opportunities for learning and dialogue, and the development of new ideas to address complex policy questions.

Pew Research Center

901 E St. NW
Suite 300
Washington, DC 20004
202-419-4300
info@pewresearch.org
www.pewresearch.org

The Pew Research Center is a nonpartisan think tank that informs the public about the issues, attitudes, and trends shaping the world. It conducts public opinion polling, demographic research, content analysis and other data-driven social science research. It does not take policy positions but rather generates a foundation of facts that enriches the public discourse and supports sound decision-making. It is nonprofit, nonpartisan, and nonadvocacy, and it values independence, objectivity, accuracy, rigor, humility, transparency, and innovation.

U.S. Department of Justice

950 Pennsylvania Avenue NW
Washington, DC 20530
202-514-2000
www.justice.gov

The U.S. Department of Justice has a mission to uphold the rule of law, protect civil rights, and keep America safe. Individuals may also take action using links on the main page to report crimes, report missing persons, find help for victims, and other actions.

Bibliography of Books

Ayad Akhtar. *Homeland Elegies*. New York, NY: Little, Brown and Company, 2020.

Jonathan Blitzer. *Everyone Who Is Gone Is Here: The United States, Central America, and the Making of a Refugee Crisis*. New York, NY: Penguin Press, 2024.

Gabriella Garcia. *Of Women and Salt*. New York, NY: Flatiron Books, 2021.

Karen Gonzalez. *The God Who Sees: Immigrants, the Bible, and the Journey to Belong*. Harrisonburg, VA: Herald Press, 2019.

Jessica Goudeau. *After the Last Border: Two Families and the Story of Refuge in America*. New York, NY: Viking, 2020.

Jay Caspian Kang. *The Loneliest Americans*. New York, NY: Crown, 2021.

Dina Nayeri. *The Ungrateful Refugee: What Immigrants Never Tell You*. New York, NY: Catapult, 2019.

Brianna Nofil. *The Migrant's Jail: An American History of Mass Incarceration*. Princeton, NJ: Princeton University Press, 2024.

Sonia Shah. *The Next Great Migration*. New York, NY: Bloomsbury, 2020.

Jeffrey Soboroff. *Separated: Inside an American Tragedy*. New York, NY: Custom House, 2020.

Jose Antonio Vargas. *Dear America: Notes of an Undocumented Citizen*. New York, NY: Dey Street Books, 2018.

Karla Villavicencio. *The Undocumented Americans*. New York, NY: One World, 2020.

Qian Julie Wang. *Beautiful Country: A Memoir*. New York, NY: Doubleday, 2021.

Jia Lynn Yang. *One Mighty and Irresistible Tide: The Epic Struggle Over American Immigration, 1924-1965*. New York, NY: W.W.Norton & Company, 2020.

Javier Zamora. *Solito: A Memoir*. New York, NY: Hogarth, 2022.

Index

A

Alien and Sedition Acts, 28
Alien Enemies Act of 1798, 124–125
American Dream, 14, 22–23, 90, 97, 102
Americanization, 18, 25
asylum, 33, 38, 44–45, 48, 50, 55, 82, 104–106, 161–163

B

bilingualism, 21
Black Power movement, 20
Biden, Joe, 33, 44, 47, 50–53, 89, 123–124, 161–163
border closings, 111
border security, 47, 49, 51

C

Center for Migration Studies, 46
Chinese Exclusion Act of 1893, 27
college graduates, 21
colonization, 23, 26
conditionality of citizenship, 25
corruption, 127, 129–130, 134–136, 144
COVID-19, 50, 67, 89, 92, 95, 111, 132, 161–162
cultural assimilation, 155–159

D

decolonization, 22, 26–27
Deferred Action for Childhood Arrivals (DACA), 38, 48–49, 51, 123, 162–163
Deferred Action for Parents of Americans (DAPA), 48
Deferred Enforced Departure, 96–97
deportations, 23, 33, 38, 70, 107–109, 122, 145
Development Relief and Education for Alien Minors (DREAM) Act, 48, 96
discrimination, 105, 157
displaced families, 130
Dreamers, 78, 90, 94–95

E

economic inequality, 23, 148, 150–151
economic recovery, 92, 111
education, 40, 48, 68, 74, 76, 91, 93–94, 111–113, 115, 127, 135, 147, 158–159, 162
exploitation, 69, 133, 142

F

family separation, 49, 120, 162

Federal Bureau of Investigation (FBI), 52
14th Amendment, 77, 124

G

gang violence, 126, 128
gender-based violence, 127, 130, 135
Global Migration Center 89

H

H1B visas, 46, 112
H2A visas, 46
humanitarians, 44, 123

I

identity politics, 20, 29
Immigration and Customs Enforcement (ICE), 80–83, 122–123
immigration laws
  Immigration and Nationality Act (1965), 22, 36, 81–82
  Immigration Act of 1990, 37
Indigenous nations, 19
instability, 25, 127, 129–131
internment camps, 117

J

job opportunities, 68, 147, 151
Justice Department, 52, 123

L

labor force, 33, 39, 60–61, 66–68, 75–76, 93, 130
lawful permanent residents, 37, 39, 57, 75

M

Massachusetts Bay colony, 28
mass migrations, 23, 155, 158–159
"melting pot," 17, 21, 102
merit, 50, 73, 111–114
Migrant Protection Protocols, 50
Migration Policy Institute, 77–78
Multiculturalism, 19–21

N

National Guard, 53
nationalism, 27–29
national security, 46–47, 82
naturalization, 39, 93–95, 140
naturalized U.S. citizens, 37, 57
New American Economy, 76
"New Colossus, The," 30–31
Northern Triangle, 51, 59

O

Obama, Barack, 24, 47–49, 52, 163

occupations, 90, 111, 155, 158
oppressed groups, 20

P

patriotism, 27
Pew Research Center, 33–34, 47, 55, 77
Plymouth colony, 28
points-based system, 111–115
population, 20, 22, 25–26, 32–35, 37–40, 44–45, 51, 55–61, 67–69, 74, 76–78, 92–93, 111–112, 131–132, 155, 157, 159, 162–163

R

Reagan, Ronald, 47
refugees, 21, 27, 29, 46, 49–50, 102, 104–106
remittance, 23, 113, 127, 132–133, 135

S

Secure Communities, 52, 80

T

Temporary Protected Status, 38, 50, 90, 123
Title 42 policy, 50–51, 161–163
trauma, 28, 119–120, 135
travel bans, 49, 51

U

United Nations Universal Declaration of Human Rights, 161
Uniting for Ukraine (U4U), 55
Ursula, 117–118, 120
U.S. Customs and Border Protection, 48, 117
U.S. Department of Homeland Security (DHS), 51, 81, 83, 95, 123
U.S.-Mexico border wall, 49–51, 53

Z

zero-tolerance policy, 49, 119